# THE NEW
# CREATIVE CHRISTMAS
# BOOK

# THE NEW
# CREATIVE CHRISTMAS
# BOOK

Compiled by Jilly MacLeod

a Salamander book

Published by Salamander Books Limited
LONDON • NEW YORK

Published by Salamander Books Ltd.,
129-137 York Way,
London N7 9LG,
United Kingdom.

© Salamander Books Ltd., 1991

**ISBN 0 86101 584 3**

Distributed by Hodder and Stoughton Services,
PO Box 6, Mill Road, Dunton Green,
Sevenoaks, Kent TN13 2XX

# CREDITS

**Editor-in-Chief:** Jilly Glassborow

**Designers:** Kathy Gummer and Tony Truscott

**Photographers:** Steve Tanner and Terry Dilliway

**Typeset by:** Barbican Print and Marketing Services, London, and The Old Mill, London

**Colour Separation by:** Fotographics Ltd, London – Hong Kong, Scantrans Pte Ltd., Singapore
and Bantam Litho Ltd., England

**Printed in Italy**

# CONTENTS

# INTRODUCTION

Following on the enormous success of *The Creative Christmas Book*, Salamander has produced this colourful new edition, giving you a further 120 imaginative ideas for things to make and decorate for the Christmas season. As well as a host of Christmas tree designs, there are also garlands, wreaths and wall decorations to brighten up your home. There are plenty of ideas for the dining table as well, with over 10 stylish centrepieces and a range of festive table mats, napkin holders and place cards.

Chapter Two shows you how you can make your presents look extra special with some imaginative gift top decorations and hand-coloured giftwraps. You can even learn how to make your own greeting cards from coloured cardboard and scraps of fabric, paper, sequins and lace.

The final chapter is packed full of original ideas for making your own gifts using a wide range of craft techniques, from dried and pressed flower arranging to hand painting and soft toy making. A hand-made present is always so much more special than a purchased one, and in this section you will find something to suit any friend or relative, be it an attractive picture or frame, a bouquet of paper flowers, a potato-print cushion or a cuddly polar bear.

Create a completely festive atmosphere in your home this Christmas with some of the original and stunning ideas featured in this chapter. We show you how to decorate the focal point of the room: the Christmas tree; and, if you are tired of ordinary tinsel and baubles, we demonstrate how easy it is to exercise individual style and chic at relatively little cost. There are numerous tree decorations to make, as well as unusual festive wreaths and garlands. And for the Christmas dinner table we show you how to create place settings, place cards, and a selection of perfect centrepieces which will complete that most special of meals.

## ALL THAT GLITTERS

For a stunning effect this Christmas, choose a colour scheme for your tree and bedeck it in reds and golds, pinks and silvers, or blues and purples, matching it to the decor of your room or simply going for your favourite colours.

Alternatively, for a cool and elegant look such as that shown below, choose only translucent and pearly white decorations, allowing the natural colours of your tree to shine forth.

Of course, it can be quite a costly affair buying all the baubles and beads needed to dress a tree. By covering your tree in colourful bows cut from sparkling party fabric (see right), you can create a lavish effect as well as keep the cost down. You will need about 1.3m (4ft) each of red and gold fabric to dress a medium sized tree, cut into strips 12cm x 80cm (5in x 30in). Fold the raw edges in to the centre along the length of a strip and tie the fabric around the end of a branch, finishing off with a bow. Pull the raw edges out from inside the loops to give the bow more volume and cut the tails in a V shape. Tie as many bows as you like all over the tree, making a large double one to fit on the top. Fill in the gaps with red and gold baubles and drape gold beads elegantly around the tree to finish.

Dried flowers always look beautiful but are especially decorative at Christmas. Brighten up the Christmas tree with sprays of dried flowers tied with tartan ribbon. Choose warm red, russet and golden yellow coloured foliage and as bright a coloured tartan as you can find so that the colours will stand out against the tree. Balance the flowers amongst the branches.

Tie a larger spray upside down at the top of the tree. Next, tie together some cinnamon sticks with tartan ribbon and hang them from the branches on fine thread. As a finishing touch, hang fir cones on narrow ribbons. Stand the tree in a basketwork pot decorated with dried flower heads glued around the rim and tartan ribbon fastened with fine wire.

This tree's stunning effect is easy to achieve. Cut star shapes from silver cardboard (see template on page 92) and position them between the branches. Then make bows from pink paper rope and place them in the gaps. The trimmings can also be hung on fine thread if the branches are rather sparse. Top the tree with a large silver star, attached with a length of wire taped to the back.

For the bows, cut a 33cm (13in) length of paper rope or use a 10cm (4in) wide crepe paper strip; bend the ends to the centre and tightly bind with sticky tape. Cut a 20cm (8in) length for the tails. Bend in half and squeeze the centre, then stick behind the bow. Bind the tails to the bow with a narrow strip and trim the tail ends diagonally. To finish, cover the tub with crepe paper.

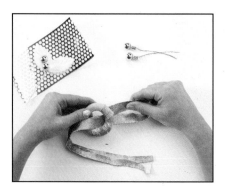

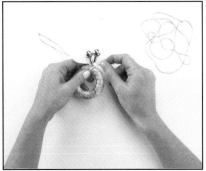

Add a touch of regal splendour to your tree with these golden decorations. To make a miniature wreath, first wind the wires of two silk leaves and two small glass balls together, and bind with white florist's tape. Cut a 16cm (6½in) length from sequin waste. Next cut a long strip of gold crepe paper, fold the edges in and bind around a small wooden ring.

Tie a loop of gold thread around the ring at the paper join. Twist the leaf and ball stems around the ring over the thread, folding in the wire ends to secure.

Fold the ends of the sequin waste into the centre so that they overlap, with the selvedges at each side. Thread a long length of fine florist's wire down the middle, through all the layers. Then thread the wire back and pull up gently to make a bow shape. Twist the wires tightly to secure and bind them around the leaf wires. Arrange the leaves, bow and balls attractively over the ring.

To make a jewelled sphere, first wrap a polystyrene ball with gold crepe paper: cut a square of paper to fit generously, and pull it up tightly over the ball. Tie firmly around the gathered paper with a length of gold thread, and knot the ends of the thread to make a hanging loop. Cut a strip of crepe paper to make a bow and fold the raw edges in. Pinch the strip into a bow shape.

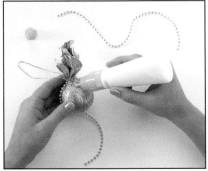

Run a line of clear adhesive around the ball and press a strip of beading trim into it. Repeat with a line of beading crossing in the opposite direction. Stick 'jewels' between the beads and large sequins, held in place with a pearl-headed pin. Trim the paper at the top of the sphere and attach the bow with a sequin trimmed pearl-headed pin.

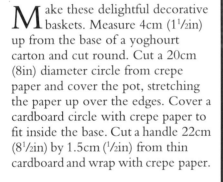

M ake these delightful decorative baskets. Measure 4cm (1½in) up from the base of a yoghourt carton and cut round. Cut a 20cm (8in) diameter circle from crepe paper and cover the pot, stretching the paper up over the edges. Cover a cardboard circle with crepe paper to fit inside the base. Cut a handle 22cm (8½in) by 1.5cm (½in) from thin cardboard and wrap with crepe paper.

From sequin foil waste cut a strip long enough to wrap around the pot. Run a line of glue along the top and bottom of the pot and in one vertical line. Wrap the foil round, pressing into the glue, and trim, straightening the overlap along the vertical line of glue. Cut two strips 5cm (2in) wide from sequin waste, fold in half, selvedges level, and cut into bow shapes.

H ere's an attractive way to add sparkle to the Christmas tree. You can buy these plain glass balls from craft suppliers, so look in craft magazines for stockists or try your nearest craft shop. As you are decorating a curved surface, it is advisable to keep the design simple. Draw the outlines of your design using a fine multi-purpose felt tip paint pen.

Try to place the motifs evenly, remembering you will see the far side of the design through the glass ball. Fill in the design with the same colour you used for the outlines. You can rub out any mistakes with a cloth soaked in turpentine.

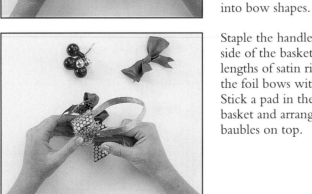

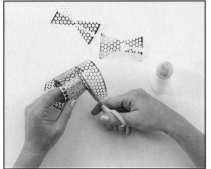

Staple the handle and foil bows each side of the basket. Tie bows from lengths of satin ribbon and stick over the foil bows with double-sided tape. Stick a pad in the bottom of the basket and arrange a bunch of glass baubles on top.

Outline your motifs in a contrasting colour, combining colours such as red and green, yellow and black, pink and purple. Add tiny dots between the motifs using the same colour as that used for the outline. Hang the baubles from your tree with gold gift wrapping thread.

# BLUE ANGEL

# CHRISTMAS STAR

Cut a 10cm (4in) diameter semi-circle of silver cardboard, silver crepe paper and crinkly film. Trim the curve of the film in zig-zags and flute the crepe paper curve between your thumb and finger. Place the crepe paper on the cardboard with the film on top and glue together along the straight edges. Overlap the straight edges in a cone and glue.

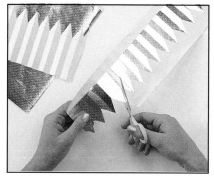

From cartridge paper cut two rectangles, one 58cm by 10cm (23in x 4in), the other 58cm by 6.5cm (23in x 2½in). Mark each one into 12mm (½in) strips and draw a line 2.5cm (1in) from the long edge. Following your marks, cut out a zig-zag edge and pleat the strips. Use spray adhesive to stick gold foil to each side of the large rectangle, and silver foil to the smaller one.

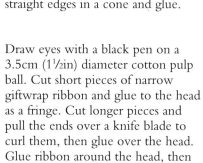
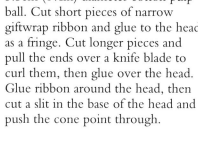

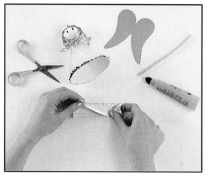

Draw eyes with a black pen on a 3.5cm (1½in) diameter cotton pulp ball. Cut short pieces of narrow giftwrap ribbon and glue to the head as a fringe. Cut longer pieces and pull the ends over a knife blade to curl them, then glue over the head. Glue ribbon around the head, then cut a slit in the base of the head and push the cone point through.

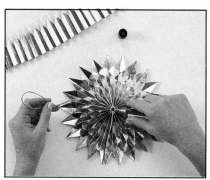

Pleat the gold strip again and fold it into a circle. Join the two ends with double-sided tape and prevent the centre from popping up by smearing glue into the centre. Weight down the star with a book until it is dry. Next make a loop from gold thread from which to hang the star, and glue this to the centre of the star at the back.

Cut silver crepe paper 11cm x 6cm (4½in x 2¼in) and flute the ends. Glue the long edges together and insert a 15cm (6in) pipecleaner for the arms through the tube and bend back the ends. Squeeze the centre and glue behind the cone, bending the arms forward. Use the template on page 93 to cut silver cardboard wings and glue them in place behind the angel.

Make up the silver star as before and place a double-sided adhesive pad on the centre back. Use this to attach the star to the gold star, aligning the pleats. Finally, put a little glue into the centre of the star and press a small glass ball in place.

Cover cotton craft ball with a double layer of nylon tights. The hole in ball should be at the neck. Cut a square of nylon and stretch over ball gathering at neck, sew through tights and bind with thread to form a neck. Trim nylon if necessary. Push neck into body gathers and sew through body and neck to secure head. Sew braid around body.

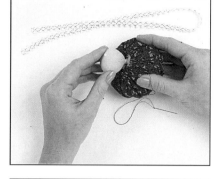

**For the girl:** Cut 20cm (8in) narrow lace. **For the clown:** Use the green ruff. Sew short edges together and gather one long edge. Place circle over head with join at the back, pull up tightly around neck and secure thread. Tie narrow ribbon around clown's neck with bow at front.

Press ½cm (¼in) to wrong side on all edges of sleeves. With wrong sides facing fold sleeve along centre length and slip stitch long edges together. Fold over 1.5cm (⅝in) at ends of pipe cleaner to make hands. Slip arms into sleeve, gather and sew fabric around wrists. Sew braid at wrists. Place arms around body with back under ruff and sew leaving front arms free.

**MATERIALS:** *Printed cotton fabric; lining fabric; white or green fabric; decorative braids, narrow lace, narrow red ribbon; 1 × 25mm (1in) diameter cotton craft ball, 2 black map pins 1 flesh colour pipe cleaner for each doll; flesh colour nylon tights; matching sewing threads; tiny red pom poms or beads; 5cm (2in) diameter circle thin card; filling; red crayon; clear drying craft glue; pinking shears*

**For either doll:** Cut body circle 18cm (7in) diameter and sleeves 13cm × 5cm (5in × 2in) in print fabric; inner Body circle 18cm (7in) diameter in lining fabric; body base circle 5cm (2in) diameter in card.
**For the girl:** Cut hat circle 8cm (3in) diameter in white fabric. **For the clown:** Cut hat (page 65) from print fabric; ruff 13cm × 2cm (5in x ¾in) in green using pinking shears.

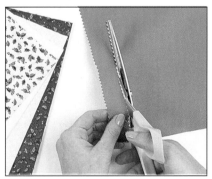

Sew lace around edge of right side of girl's hat. Sew running stitches 1.5cm (⅝in) from fabric edge to gather. Pull up stitches until hat fits head, add filling to crown and sew hat to head around gathers. Sew ribbon above gathers and tie with bow in front. Sew or glue pom pom or bead to centre of neck lace.

**For either doll:** Sew long running stitches around edge of inner body circle. Mould filling to make a ball of about 7.5cm (3in) diameter and place in centre of inner body. Pull up stitches to gather edge tightly and secure. Glue card base to cover stitches. Gather edge of body circle. Place card base to centre of wrong side of body. Pull up stitches.

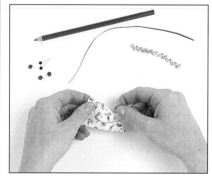

Sew clown's hat seam A–B. Turn to right side. Fill with stuffing and sew to head around edge. Sew braid to cover edge, sew or glue one pom pom or bead to front and three to body centre front. Glue back of map pins and press into head. Mark mouth in red crayon. Cut 20cm (8in) narrow ribbon, fold in centre, sew ends to body and loop to back of head to balance doll.

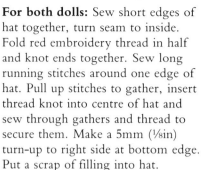

**For both dolls:** Sew short edges of hat together, turn seam to inside. Fold red embroidery thread in half and knot ends together. Sew long running stitches around one edge of hat. Pull up stitches to gather, insert thread knot into centre of hat and sew through gathers and thread to secure them. Make a 5mm (⅛in) turn-up to right side at bottom edge. Put a scrap of filling into hat.

With seam to back, fit hat onto doll. **For the boy:** Cut 10 × 1cm (⅜in) lengths of yarn, push one end of each piece under hat front. **For the girl:** Cut 4 × 2cm (¾in) lengths, push both ends of each piece under hat to form loops on centre front head. When satisfied with position remove hat and hair, spread glue onto head and arrange hair.

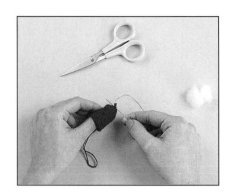

MATERIALS: *For one doll – 3 × 10cm (4in) lengths of pipe cleaners, red if possible; 20mm (¾in) diameter polished wooden bead; 2 × 10mm (⅜in) diameter polished wooden beads; red, green, white and brown felts; matching sewing threads; 25cm (10in) red soft embroidery thread; narrow gold ric-rac braid; narrow lace edging (girl); brown knitting yarn; tiny bead for brooch (girl); soft filling; strong clear adhesive; red and black, fine-tip, permanent marker pens; tracing paper*

When glue is dry mark features onto doll with pencil before using the black pen for the eyes and the red for the mouth. Also colour cheeks red for the boy. Allow features to dry then glue edge of hat and place onto head over hair ends.

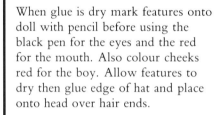

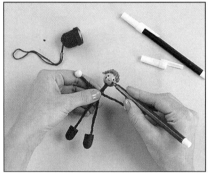

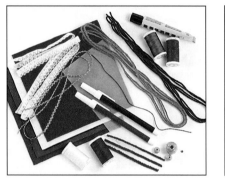

Trace actual size patterns. To make body and head for either doll, squeeze glue into hole of the 20mm (¾in) bead. Hold two pipe cleaners side by side with ends even and push one end of pair halfway into bead. Glue feet together in pairs with opposite ends of a pipe cleaner between each pair – the curved edges of feet make toes of doll.

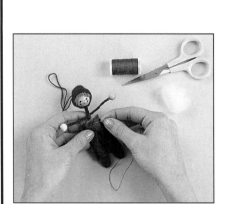

Oversew boy's trouser pieces together at sides A–B and inside leg seams C–D–C. Turn to right side out, easing through legs. Fit onto doll, add a scrap of filling to body of trousers and sew to pipe cleaners around waist. Make and fit girl's pantaloons in same way, then gather them at ankles and sew or glue lace to right side above gathers.

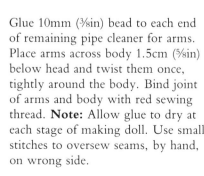

Glue 10mm (⅜in) bead to each end of remaining pipe cleaner for arms. Place arms across body 1.5cm (⅝in) below head and twist them once, tightly around the body. Bind joint of arms and body with red sewing thread. **Note:** Allow glue to dry at each stage of making doll. Use small stitches to oversew seams, by hand, on wrong side.

Cut boy's jacket for neck and front opening on solid lines E–E–J. Fold across shoulders N–N and sew side and underarm seams matching letters. Turn jacket through to right side out. Ease bead hands through arms to fit jacket onto the doll. Overlap fronts at neck and sew together between dots. Push scraps of filling under jacket around front and back shoulders.

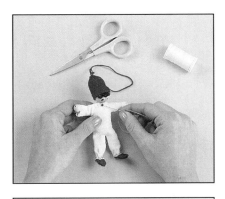

Cut a scrap of gold braid and glue to front. Fold feet to front at right angles to legs. Make girl's blouse in same way as jacket. Fit onto doll with opening at back. Add filling, overlap complete back opening and sew together. Gather and sew lower edge over pantaloon waist. Glue lace around neck and wrists and sew brooch bead to lace at front neck.

Glue or sew lace on wrong side to show below one long edge of skirt. On right side glue gold braid above bottom edge. Sew short skirt edges together. Sew long running stitches to gather waist. Fit skirt onto doll with seam at centre back and sew gathered edge to blouse at a high waistline. Glue or sew waistband, with join at back, to cover gathers.

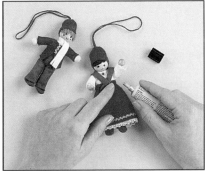

Cut a fringe at scarf ends, tie scarf around boy's neck, glue one end to jacket front and leave other end free. Wrap shawl around girl, cross ends and glue in front.

Decorations only – not recommended for young children

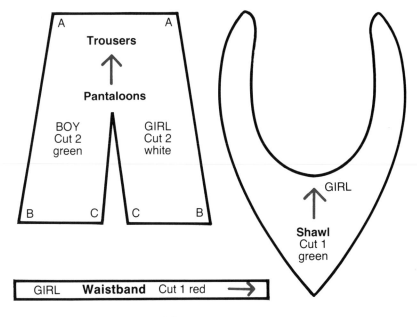

**Trousers**

↑

**Pantaloons**

BOY
Cut 2
green

GIRL
Cut 2
white

A          A
B  C    C  B

GIRL   **Waistband**   Cut 1 red →

Actual height of dolls: 11cm (4¼in)

BOY **Scarf** Cut 1 white ↓

**Foot**
Cut 4
brown
↓

M          H

K    L        F    G

**Jacket/Blouse**
BOY  Cut 1 red
GIRL  Cut 1 white

N    E———E    N ↑

K    L        F    G

M    J    H

**Shawl**
Cut 1
green

↑ GIRL

**Hat**
Cut 1 red
←

**Skirt**
Cut 1 red
←

# WOVEN CIRCLES

# FELT HEARTS

Interweave red and green felt shapes to form hearts, adding glittery beads and sequins. Cut two templates (see page 92) from thin cardboard. Stick green felt onto one side of a template and trim to the card edges. Cut along the marked slits. Cover the opposite side of the template with green felt in the same way. Repeat the procedure, covering the second template with red felt.

Interlock the two shapes together by weaving the strips over and under their opposite number to form a heart shape.

Use shiny strands of raffia and plastic canvas circles (available from craft shops) to create these unusual tree ornaments. Weave raffia over the inner half of a 7.5cm (3in) circle with straight stitches, working each quarter section from the same central hole. The stitches will look the same from either side.

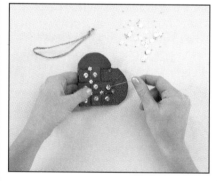

Punch a hole centrally in the top of the heart; thread with a 20cm (8in) length of gold cord and tie into a loop. Finally, decorate each side of the heart with sequins and beads; either glue or handsew them in place.

Work the outer half of the circle in the same way using the second colour. Blanket stitch around the outer edge of the circle using the same colour as the centre, tying the ends to form a loop.

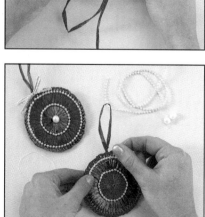

On each side, handsew pearl bead trim between the two halves of the straight stitches and around the outer edge. Sew a pearl button to the centre on each side. To finish, tie a silver ribbon bow around the base of the loop.

**R**ing out the bells this Christmas from the tree tops. Using the pattern on page 92, cut out three side panel pieces from each of two festive fabrics. Pin and stitch the panels together, with right sides facing, to form a ring, alternating the fabrics. Cut an 8cm (3⅛in) diameter circle for the base and, with right sides facing, sew in place.

Turn the bell the right side out through the open end and fill with shredded wadding. Turn in the top raw edges and work a gathering stitch around the top; pull up tight to close and fasten off. Cut a 4.5cm (1¾in) diameter red felt circle for the clapper. Sew running stitch around the outer edge; fill with wadding and gather into a ball; fasten off. Stitch the clapper to the centre of the base.

To decorate the bell, stitch bead trim over the seamlines, beginning and ending at the edge of the base. Finally, tie a 50cm (20in) length of ribbon into a loop and tie the ends into a bow; sew onto the top of the bell.

**E**ight-pointed stars are a traditional Christmas design. For each side of a star, cut eight diamonds from iron-on interfacing (see page 92 for pattern). Cut two diamonds from each of four fabrics, adding a seam allowance. Fuse interfacings to the fabric diamonds and tack (baste) the raw edges over the interfacing. Oversew the diamonds together to form a star.

Make up two sides in this way and place with wrong sides facing; slip-stitch the outer edges together. Sew four lengths of braid across the seamlines, finishing one off to form a hanging loop. Finally, sew a pearl button to each point and to each indent.

Cut a 3cm (1¼in) square of cardboard to use as a template for the doors. Draw around the square twenty-three times on the back of the tree, positioning the doors at random but leaving the trunk clear. Cut three sides of the doors, leave the right hand side 'hinged' so the door opens the right way on the other side.

On the right side of the tree, score the hinged side of each door lightly so it will open easily – but do not open the doors yet. Number the doors one to twenty-three with a silver pen.

Cut out small Christmas pictures from wrapping paper and used greeting cards. On the back of the tree, stick each picture behind a door by spreading paper glue on the tree around the doors.

Decorate the calendar with a gold star on the top and circles of metallic cardboard between the doors.

Write the number twenty-four on the front of a small red gift box with a silver pen. Stick a ribbon rosette on the top and glue the box onto the tree trunk. Fill the box with sweets. To finish, stick a picture hanger on the back of the calendar at the top.

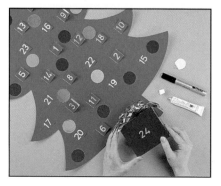

This Advent calendar can be used every year at Christmas. First make the Christmas tree pattern. Cut a piece of paper measuring about 63cm x 50cm (25in x 20in) and fold in half lengthwise. Draw half the tree with a trunk against the foldline and cut it out. Open out flat and use the pattern as a template to cut out the tree in green cardboard.

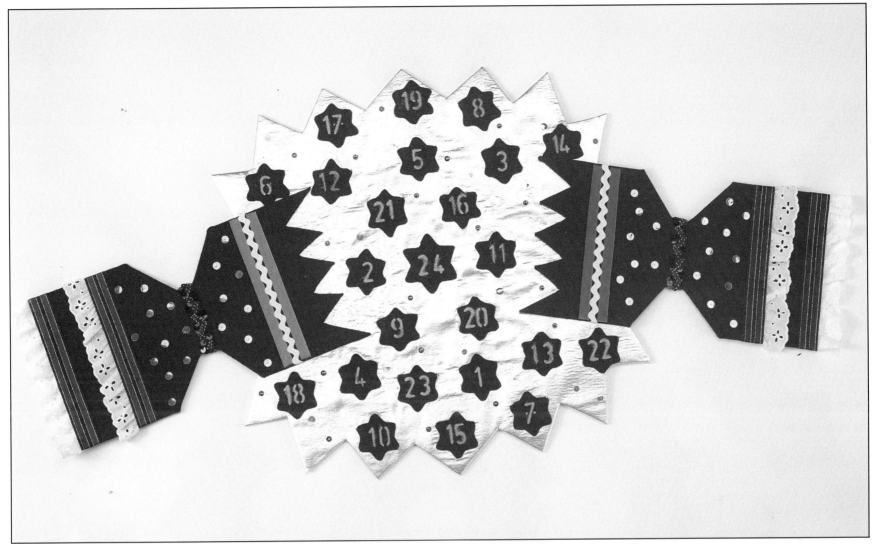

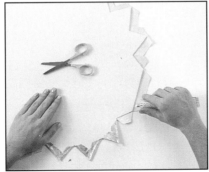

Eat a chocolate a day until Christmas! Use the template on page 94 to cut out a cardboard star and iron-on interfacing. Cut out a silver fabric star, adding a 12mm (½in) allowance all around. Iron the interfacing centrally to the wrong side of the silver fabric. Cut out 24 red felt stars, making one larger, and stitch to the silver background, leaving the tops open.

Position the cardboard star centrally over the wrong side of the silver fabric. Trim the fabric allowance away at the corners and the edges over onto the cardboard, sticking in place with glue.

Cut two cardboard cracker ends, using the template on page 94. Cover with red felt, cut 12mm (½in) larger all around, gluing the raw edges over to the wrong side as before. Decorate with rows of braid, ribbons and sequins.

Position a spare piece of cardboard in each red 'pocket' in turn and stencil on a number using a silver pen and plastic stencil. Stick the cracker ends on either side of the silver star, and glue sequins between the pockets to decorate. Finally, pop a silver chocolate coin in each pocket.

Deck the hall with sprigs of holly, made from felt and suspended from tartan ribbon. Make a holly pattern from paper and cut out two pieces of green felt and one of wadding for every sprig. Place two felt pieces together, with wadding in between, and pin in place. Overstitch all around the edges with embroidery thread.

Measure a length of tartan ribbon from which to hang the holly. Now cut shorter lengths to make the bows. Tie the sprigs to the garland with the short ribbons, finishing off with a bow. Finally, cut a V in the tails of the bows and hang your garland in place.

Thread your sewing machine with green cotton thread and stitch 'veins' onto each holly leaf – one down the centre and the rest sloping from the centre to the points. Next, take four red wooden or plastic beads for each leaf and sew them in place, close to the inside edge, using six strands of red embroidery thread.

This garland is made from different coloured tissue paper stars. Refer to the template on page 93 to make the basic pattern. Fold up six layers of tissue paper into quarters, place a quarter of the paper pattern on top, edges level and cut out. Fold the tissue paper in half again, (separate some of the layers if too bulky) and cut two slits in the positions marked in the photograph below. Cut a collection of different coloured tissue paper 'stars' in this way, plus two stars cut from cartridge paper for the garland ends. Glue a tissue star to each paper star using spray adhesive. Stick a small piece of double-sided tape to the centre of one tissue star and press this onto the centre of the tissue-covered paper star.

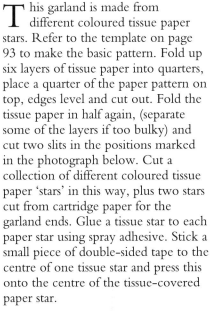

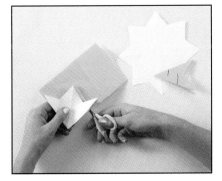

Next place double-sided tape on four opposite points of the tissue star, and stick another star on top, aligning the points and slits. Keep repeating the sequence, pressing pieces of double-sided tape alternately to the centre, then to the four points, of each star, building up the layers until the garland is the required length. Finish by attaching the other end section.

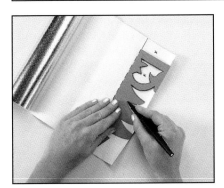

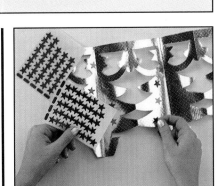

Use this attractive frieze to decorate shelves, or to hang along a wall. From a length of foil gift wrap cut a long strip 23cm (9in) wide. Make a tree template from paper using the pattern on page 93 and line it up along one short edge of the gift wrap. Draw around the outline marking a fold line down the centre of the tree shape. Mark an X on each section to be cut out.

Fold the gift wrap concertina fashion along its length and staple the layers together above and below the pattern area to prevent the folds from slipping. Cut out through all the layers, using a craft knife to cut out the enclosed areas between the star and the bell shapes. Be careful not to cut through the folds at the edge.

Open the frieze out. The foil can be left in gentle folds, or pressed flat with a cool iron. Stick self-adhesive foil stars all over the trees. You can make the frieze to the required length simply by joining several frieze strips together end to end, with sticky tape.

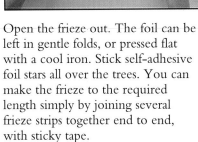

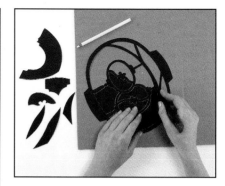

Hang this Oriental mobile at a window this Christmas and watch the winter sun shine through the coloured tissue paper. Use the template on page 92 to cut out a pair of lanterns in black cardboard. Cut out all the sections, taking care not to cut through any of the 'bridges'.

To achieve the stained glass effect, cut out coloured tissue paper a little larger than the sections to be covered. Glue the pieces of tissue paper to the back of one lantern. Trim the edges. Glue a silky red tassel to hang from the bottom of one lantern at the centre. Now glue the two lanterns together enclosing the tissue paper. Suspend the mobile on red embroidery thread.

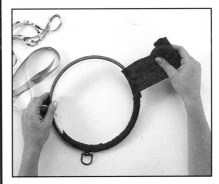

Pull the cord and watch Santa dance. Use the template on page 93 to cut out the cardboard pieces. Cut one body and a pair of arms and legs from red cardboard. Mark the crosses on the back. Cut a pink face and glue to the head. Cut a white hat brim and beard, bobble and two cuffs. Glue the hat brim and beard over the face and the bobble to the top of the hat.

Add some Christmas cheer with this festive ring. Cut a strip of crepe paper the length of the roll and bind a 20cm (8in) embroidery ring, securing the ends with double-sided tape near the hanging loop. Cut narrow gold ribbon about 110cm (43in) long and wind around the ring, securing with tape. Cut the same length from a gold sequin strip and wind between the ribbon.

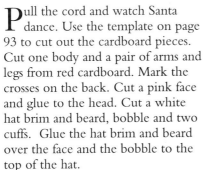

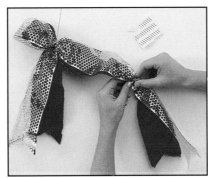

Cut out two green mittens, a black belt and two boots. Butt the straight ends of the mittens and arms together and glue cuffs over the joins. Wrap gold sticky tape around the middle of the belt and glue to the body. Glue the boot tops under the legs. Cut out a pink nose and glue on the face. Draw the eyes and mouth with felt-tipped pens.

Cut crepe paper 1m (40in) long and 20cm (8in) wide; fold in half lengthways. Cut the same length from sequin waste and place over the crepe strip. Bind the centre with a long piece of florists' wire and trim ends into a V shape. Measure 23cm (9in) each side of the centre, bind with wire and fold the strip into a bow, lining up the wired points. Secure with a double-sided adhesive pad.

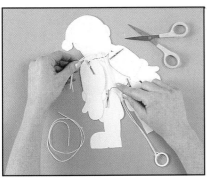

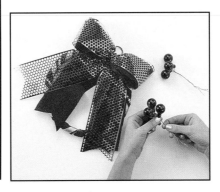

Mark dots on the limbs and attach to the body with paper fasteners at the crosses. Pull the limbs downwards on the back and tie the arms together with thread fastened through the dots. Tie the legs in the same way Thread a small ring onto a double length of fine cord. Knot the cord around the legs' thread and then the arms' thread.

Use the trailing centre wires to secure the bow in position at the ring and arrange the ribbon ends over the ring. Finally, wire three small glass balls together and wrap these around the bow centre.

**P**ick glittery fabrics and Christmas prints for this simple but effective wreath. Cut out lots of 8cm (3¼in) fabric squares with pinking shears. Cut a 10cm (4in) length of wire and thread a 1cm (³⁄₈in) glass bead in the centre. Pinch a square of fabric together across the diagonal and bend the wire in half across it, twisting the ends together to secure. Repeat for the other fabric squares.

Press the decorations into a dry foam polystyrene wreath, covering it completely (above). To finish, form a double bow from 3.5 cm (1½in) wide silver ribbon and secure onto the ring with wired beads (below). Cut the ribbon ends into Vs.

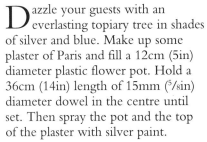

Dazzle your guests with an everlasting topiary tree in shades of silver and blue. Make up some plaster of Paris and fill a 12cm (5in) diameter plastic flower pot. Hold a 36cm (14in) length of 15mm (⅝in) diameter dowel in the centre until set. Then spray the pot and the top of the plaster with silver paint.

Wind an 80cm (32in) length of silver ribbon around the dowel, fastening both ends with double-sided adhesive tape. Push a 20cm (8in) diameter florists' dry foam ball centrally on to the top of the dowel, gouging a hole in the ball first with a craft knife.

Next, make up a selection of decorations from natural materials. Stick short lengths of wire into walnuts and spray them silver. Wind lengths of wire around the base of some fir cones and spray the tips of the cones silver. Cut cinnamon sticks into 5cm (2in) lengths, wire them into bundles of three or four, then wrap the bundles with knotted silver cord to cover the wire.

Using pinking shears, cut out 10cm (4in) squares of glittery and tartan fabrics. Cut a 20cm (8in) length of wire; fold evenly in half across the diagonal of a fabric square, pinching the fabric together, then twist the ends of the wire secure. Repeat for the other fabric pieces. Stick glittery balls onto short lengths of wire.

Press the decorations into the ball until it is completely covered. We have also added artificial berries, silver acorns, wire springs and poppy seed heads. Cover an earthenware flower pot with fabric using PVA adhesive, finishing at the top with a strip of silver ribbon and a bow. Fit the plastic pot inside and a double bow of silver and tartan ribbon around the centre of the stalk.

Hang this delightful garland on a door for a warm Christmas welcome to your visitors. Wrap four small boxes with red foil giftwrap and trim with narrow gold giftwrapping ribbon. Bend lengths of stub wire in half and thread through the ribbon on the underside.

Position the boxes evenly spaced around a florists' dry foam ring , pushing the wires into the ring to secure. Next, wire some large fir cones and Chinese lanterns ready to insert into the ring. To wire a Chinese lantern, place a stub wire against the stem and carefully bind them together with florists' reel wire close to the top. Break off the extending end of the stem.

Fill in between the gift boxes with the fir cones and Chinese lanterns, along with dried helichrysum (strawflowers or everlasting), wired in the same way as the Chinese lanterns. Also insert some seed pods. Gradually cover the whole ring, filling in any gaps with smaller fir cones, flowers and seed pods. When complete, the garland can be hung on two large nails 4cm (1⅝in) apart.

Cut two pieces of red crepe paper 50cm x 32cm (19½ x 12½in). Fold a long edge under 2cm (¾in) then fold in half lengthways. Bend the ends of one piece to the centre to form a bow and bind with sticky tape. Glue the long edges of the last piece together, pleat the centre and stick behind the bow. Bind the centre with a strip of crepe paper and wire the bow to the ring.

# HOLLY WREATH

Hang this everlasting wreath on the door for a warm welcome to your visitors. Cut 5cm (2in) squares of green crepe paper and stick a small piece of masking tape in the centre for extra strength. Cut the point off a cocktail stick and use to make holes in a polystyrene ring. Push each square into a hole with the blunt end of the stick.

Continue pushing in squares until the ring is hidden. Take some artificial red berries on wires and push them into the wreath at random to decorate.

Tie a large bow of red satin ribbon. Bend a length of wire into a 'U' shape and thread through the back of the bow. Push the ends of the wire into the wreath.

This unusual and imaginative wreath makes a striking decoration to hang on the door during the festive season. To create it, you will first need to buy a twig wreath from your local florist. Begin the arrangement by wiring small bunches of oak leaves together. Also take a few pieces of sponge mushroom and push wires through one side.

Attach the leaves and fungus to the wreath, forming three groups evenly spaced around the ring. Now wire up some lotus seedheads - wiring the large ones singly and the small ones in groups of two or three. Insert these in amongst the other plants.

Push short lengths of wire as far as they will go through one end of some walnuts. Form small groups of about three to four nuts each by twisting the wires together. Slot the walnuts into the three groups of plants. Next add a few witch hazel twigs, allowing them to break out of the arrangement and cover some bare patches between the groups.

To finish, wire together several bunches of yarrow and slot them into the arrangement, using them to close up the gaps slightly between the three main groups. The yarrow adds necessary colour to the wreath and brings it to life.

T his sophisticated garland makes a stunning decoration to hang on a wall or sit on a side table. Insert four pairs of large dried flowers (we have used Carlisle thistles) evenly spaced apart in a florists' dry foam ring. Arrange white sea lavender between the flowers, virtually covering the ring.

Next, insert some cream-coloured teasels, followed by gold sprayed seed pods, artificial leaves and large wired fir cones, evenly spread throughout the garland.

Any gaps can be filled with cream helichrysum (strawflowers or everlasting) and small seed pods and fir cones. To wire the flowers, place a stub wire against the stem and bind them together close to the top with reel wire. Break off the extending end of the stem.

# GOLD AND SILVER

# FESTIVE GARLAND

A silver bowl bursting with roses and freesias makes the perfect centrepiece for the festive season. Fill the bowl with water. Then cut short the stems of the cream spider chrysanthemums (to around 5cm, 2in) and pack into the bowl's wire mesh centre – these will give depth to the final arrangement.

Place yellow roses in between the chrysanthemums, keeping the stems slightly longer. Next, intersperse the arrangement with a few freesias.

Finally, place *Leucodendron* and freesia buds among the display, ensuring the stems are slightly longer than those of the other flowers; these will provide a stark contrast to the gold and silver. For a short period of time, such as during a dinner party, a full blown rose at the foot of the bowl will complete the picture, though, out of the water, the bloom's lifespan will be limited.

Bring your table to life with this attractive floral candle ring. Stick double-sided tape around the outside edge of a sponge ring mould. Adhere pleated green cellophane to this and secure with a little more sticky tape. This creates an attractive trim and is an alternative to foliage.

Insert chunks of soaked florists' foam into the ring, placing slightly thicker pieces at the back. Working around the ring insert short stems of daisy chrysanthemums to complete the circle.

Throughout the chrysanthemums dot blue-dyed yarrow and some little gold-sprayed cones on wires. Three white candles complete the garland. (The non-drip variety are best for a floral arrangement.)

# SUMPTUOUS

# FIRE AND ICE

T his sumptuous arrangement of plump flowers on a green glass cake stand looks almost edible! Place a round piece of soaked florists' foam in the centre of the stand. Then use yellow roses and alstroemeria alternately, cutting the stems on a slant and keeping them short so that once inserted into the foam the flower heads rest on the edge of the dish.

Finally, top the arrangement with a few sprays of mimosa which will retain its pretty fluffy heads longer if conditioned first. This is done by submerging flower heads under cold water then dipping stems into 2.5cm (1in) of boiling water for a few seconds. Stand in a jug of warm water until the flowers have dried off.

The next layer comprises the bobbly 'flowers' of *Leucodendron brunia* followed by a ring of Persian buttercups. The latter will last longer if their stems are put into boiling water for a few seconds, before being given a long drink.

A shallow ovenware dish forms the base for this arrangement of fiery chrysanthemums, carnations and capsicums (appropriately known as Christmas pepper in the United States). Place soaked florists' foam into the dish and cover with *Viburnum tinus* allowing the stems to escape over the sides of the dish.

To create the focal point of the arrangement, take six full blooming orange carnations and arrange them uniformly across the outline.

Fill in the outline with greenish white spray chrysanthemums. Their colour provides a dramatic contrast to the orange carnations, and their flame-shaped petals aptly fit the theme of the arrangement. Complete the display with capsicums, taking them through and along the length of the arrangement.

H ere is an exotic arrangement to grace the supper table. Cut a slice of florists' foam and glue to the centre of a plastic plate, then trim away the upper edges diagonally. Dampen the foam. Push three candle holders into the top, forming a ring, and insert three white candles of varying heights. Arrange short lengths of trailing ivy to hide the holders.

Push large ivy leaves into the foam to cover the plate as shown above then arrange apples on cocktail sticks around the foam. Next, place small bunches of grapes between the apples, securing them to the foam with stub wires bent in half. Fill any gaps with chincherinchee flowers and individual grapes on cocktail sticks as shown below. Be sure to wash the fruit afterwards if you intend to eat it.

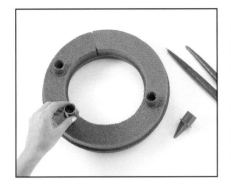

This festive table centrepiece is inexpensive to produce as the foliage used can be found in abundance during the Christmas period. Take a florists' foam ring and insert four candle holders evenly spaced around it.

Dampen the ring and insert four red candles in the holders. We have used hand-made candles for added interest. Now push sprigs of yew into the ring, positioning all the foliage in the same direction.

Next, take four large fir cones and bind wire around the base between the lower scales leaving a long length of wire to insert into the ring. Push the cone wires into the ring between the candles.

Finally, add sprigs of holly and berries to the ring. Berries can be added separately to add colour evenly throughout the decoration. Artificial berries can be used if real ones are not available.

# VINE GARLAND CANDLE RING

Gold and silver look stunning by candlelight and this festive arrangement will flatter any table setting. To begin, spray a vine garland with gold paint, sprinkle with gold glitter, and leave to dry.

Take three flat-based candle holders and stick florists' fixative putty under each one. Position them evenly around the garland, using florists' wire to secure each holder firmly in place.

To make the silver roses cut strips of silver crepe paper 53cm (21in) by 9cm (3½in). Fold in half lengthways and tuck the short ends in. Run double-sided tape along the lower edge of a folded strip and place a wired group of gold balls at one end. Roll the crepe paper around the balls, pinching the paper tightly together at the base. Finally, crimp the petal edges to curve outwards.

Stick a double-sided adhesive pad to the base of each rose and position four flowers around each candle holder. Cut 23cm (9in) lengths of gold ribbon and fold into double loops. Secure the ends with florists' wire and stick between the roses using adhesive pads. Tease the rose petals and gold loops to shape to hide the holders and put candles in place.

$A$dorn the New Year dinner table with this attractive centrepiece. Cut a length of crepe paper 120cm x 20cm (48in x 8in). Stick the ends together on the wrong side with clear sticky tape. Place a 25cm (10in) diameter polystyrene ring in the middle and sew the long edges of crepe paper together with a running stitch enclosing the polystyrene ring. Gather up the seam and fasten off.

Spray five candle holders white and push into the ring evenly spaced apart. Then drape strings of white pearls and narrow green coiled giftwrapping ribbon around the ring, gluing the ends to the underside.

Stick two rectangles of metallic blue cardboard back to back with spray adhesive and cut out five masks using the template on page 93. Score gently along the fold line of the tabs with a craft knife and bend the tabs backwards. Stick each mask by the tabs, in front of a candle.

Glue tiny blue and green star-shaped sequins to the ring, then cut out ten small stars from silver cardboard and glue between the candles and to each mask. Finally, place silver candles in the holders.

Fill this sleigh with foil wrapped candies for a charming table centrepiece. Apply gold embossed paper to both sides of thick cardboard with spray glue and cut a pair of sleighs using the template on page 93. For the base, glue gold paper to both sides of a rectangle of thin cardboard 36cm x 16cm (14$\frac{1}{8}$in x 6$\frac{1}{4}$in).

Mark the broken lines on the sleighs. Score along the base 1.5cm ($\frac{5}{8}$in) from each long edge. Snip away tiny triangles up to the scored lines so that the base will bend easily. Bend the snipped edge backwards at right angles.

Glue the snipped edges between the sleighs along the broken lines and lower, straight edges. Use the template to cut out two flowers in red foil paper and two leaves in green. Glue two leaves under each flower and glue three sequins in the middle. Glue a flower to each side of the sleigh and line it with scrunched up iridescent film.

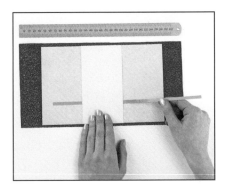

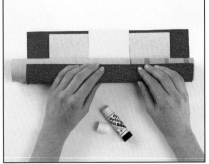

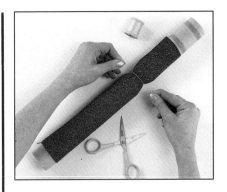

It is easy and economical to make crackers. Cut crepe paper 32cm x 16cm (12³⁄₄in x 6¹⁄₄in), keeping the grain of the paper parallel with the long sides. Lay a piece of thin writing paper 24cm x 15cm (9¹⁄₂in x 6in) centrally on top. Next cut thin cardboard 15cm x 8cm (6in x 3in) and lay it across the centre. Slip a cracker snap underneath.

Take two cardboard tubes, the sort found inside rolls of kitchen towel, and cut one in half. Lay the long tube on the lower edge of the crepe paper, with the end level with the cardboard edge. Butt a short tube against the long one and roll up tightly. Glue the overlapped edges of paper together with a low-tack adhesive.

Pull the short tube out for 5cm (2in) and tie thread tightly around the cracker between the tubes. Push the tubes together again then remove the short tube. Drop a gift, motto and paper hat inside and pull out the long tube a further 12.5cm (5in) . Tie thread tightly between the tube and cardboard inside the cracker. Untie the threads.

Cut two 25cm (10in) lengths of gold filigree lace – the kind that has a drawstring thread along one edge. Gather up the drawstring and tie the lace around the necks of the cracker. Gently stretch the ends of the cracker to flute the edges. Remove the drawstring from a length of lace and glue around the middle of the cracker. Glue a dried flower to the cracker to complete.

A plain wooden candlestick can be decorated very effectively with pressed flowers. Begin by coating the candleholder with 'two pack' gloss varnish. While the varnish is still tacky, adhere sprays of foliage (we have used that of *Ranunculus* 'Bachelor's Buttons') to both back and front of the holder. Leave to dry.

Re-varnish the holder and centre a spray of montbretia buds on top of the foliage (see above). Add larger, single buds towards the base. While this second coat of varnish is still sticky, fix a cream potentilla in the centre of each design (see below). Leave the holder to dry completely before finishing with two thin coats of gloss varnish.

T hese delicate pressed flower designs transform ordinary thick candles. But be very careful not to let the candle burn down below the protective film, as the designs are not flameproof! For the yellow candle fix narrow leaves in a spray with latex adhesive (we have used autumn sumach). Repeat twice around the candle.

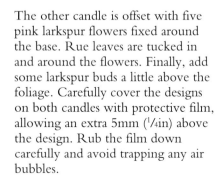

The other candle is offset with five pink larkspur flowers fixed around the base. Rue leaves are tucked in and around the flowers. Finally, add some larkspur buds a little above the foliage. Carefully cover the designs on both candles with protective film, allowing an extra 5mm (¼in) above the design. Rub the film down carefully and avoid trapping any air bubbles.

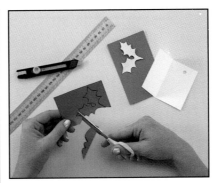

Miniature holly sprigs give a festive touch to a place card. From thin cardboard cut a rectangle 7.5cm x 10cm (3in x 4in). Gently score across the centre, using a craft knife against a ruler, and fold the card in half. Punch a hole in the lower left side. Make a holly leaf template from thick paper and draw around the edge on to thick green paper (artist's Canson paper is ideal). Cut out.

Score lightly down the centre of each leaf and bend to shape. Bind a bunch of red flower stamens (available from craft shops) together with fine florists' wire and cut in half across the stems to create two bunches. Bind the stamens to the front of the leaves with red florists' tape.

Fold a short length of narrow curling ribbon in half, at a slight angle, and secure fold with a small piece of double-sided tape. Curl the ribbon against a scissor blade and stick to front of the holly sprig. Write the name on the card and push the holly sprig through the punched hole, securing the stems to the back of the card with a small piece of sticky tape.

Choose a simple motif, such as holly, mistletoe, or bells, and create your own unique festive tea service. For this attractive holly design, you will need plain white china, red and green ceramic paint and a fine paint brush. Paint the outlines of the holly leaves with green paint, grouping the leaves together in threes. Now fill in the leaf outlines with more green paint.

Join up the leaves with garlands of red berries made by applying dots of red ceramic paint with a very fine brush. Also add clusters of berries at the base of the leaves. When the paint is completely dry, finish off with a coat of ceramic varnish. To complete the picture, you can even paint the motif on to the corner of your paper napkins.

Christmas colours are woven together to make a matching table mat and napkin set. From cartridge paper cut out a rectangle

37cm x 27cm (14½in x 10½in) and mark a 2.5cm (1in) border all round. Draw lines 12mm (½in) apart across the paper. Cut a piece of sticky-backed velour fabric a little larger all round and peel off the backing paper. Lay the the rectangle centrally on top and, using a craft knife, cut through the drawn lines as shown. Fold overlapping fabric over and stick down.

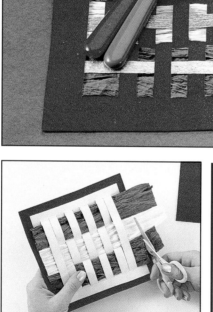

Weave lengths of green and white paper ribbon through the cut strips, arranging the ribbon so both ends pass under the border. Fold gold and silver crepe paper into narrow strips and weave over the green and white ribbon. Hold the strips in place with a little double-sided tape at both ends. Trim away the excess paper, then cover the back of the mat with sticky-backed fabric.

Cut a coaster mat from cartridge paper 17cm (6½in) square. Make a border as for the table mat, and mark, cover and cut in the same way. Weave with two lengths of each colour and cover the back with sticky-backed fabric as before.

To make the napkin ring cut a strip from cartridge paper 17cm x 6.5cm (6½in x 2½in). Mark out a 12mm (½in) border and divide into strips 12mm (½in) apart. Cover with sticky-backed fabric, and cut strips as before. Weave green ribbon and silver or gold crepe through the slits and secure with double-sided tape. Cut a length of fabric for the backing and stick in place.

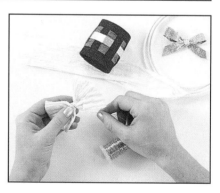

Join the two ends of the ring with double-sided tape. Make a bow shape from white paper ribbon, binding the centre with fine florists' wire. Make a small bow shape from folded gold crepe paper and stick across the white bow with double-sided tape. Stick the completed bow over the join in the napkin ring using double-sided tape.

# CHRISTMAS BASKET

# SANTA NAPKIN RINGS

For an unusual centrepiece, fill a basket with festive fabric balls. Cut a holly leaf shape from medium weight interfacing. Cut a strip of fabric twice the length of the leaf and stitch the interfacing to the wrong side. Fold the fabric over the leaf and stitch over the previous stitches. Cut out with pinking shears. Make three more leaves, add beads for berries and sew to the basket.

Make up a 3cm (1¼in) wide frill by cutting a fabric strip twice the length of the basket top by 8cm (3¼in). With wrong sides together, fold in half lengthways so raw edges overlap in the centre; sew running stitches along the length and gather. Pull up to fit the top of the basket and handsew in position, neatening the ends together. Wrap glittery cord around the basket handle.

For each ball, cut a 20cm (8in) fabric circle with pinking shears. Wrap around a 5cm (2in) compressed paper ball, pleating up the fabric evenly. Cut a 25cm (10in) length of ribbon; gather along one edge with running stitch, pull into a rosette and fasten off. Pin to the top of the ball, through all layers of fabric, with a glass-headed pin threaded through a star-shaped sequin.

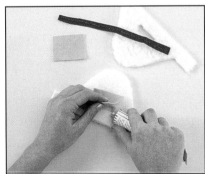

Lay a festive table with a cheery napkin ring for each guest. Cut out one pattern piece (see page 92) from white fur fabric, a piece of flesh-coloured felt 5.5cm x 4.5cm (2¼in x 1¾in), and a 15cm x 1cm (6in x ⅜in) strip of red felt. Stick the flesh-coloured felt centrally across the back of the opening on the fur fabric to form the face.

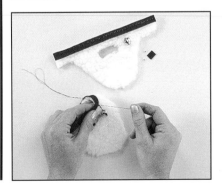

Now glue the red felt strip across the top of the fur fabric piece. Stick on two small eyes and a square of red felt for the nose. Fold the side panels back to form a ring, overlapping them by 1cm (⅜in), and glue. Finally fasten a bell to one side of the red band with a length of 'worked' thread, sewing a few strands between the band and the bell and working over them with buttonhole stitch.

B e the belle of the ball with a lavishly jewelled mask. Spray glue two pieces of gold cardboard together for extra strength, then use the template on page 93 to cut out the mask. Stick double-sided tape to the top edge on the back of the mask. Cut a strip of iridescent film 50cm x 6cm (20in x 2¼in). Scrunch up one long edge and press onto the tape.

Glue an iridescent plastic flower to the left-hand corner. Glue small glass stones at random to the mask and stick one in the centre of the flower. A pair of tweezers is useful for holding tiny stones. Glue gold plastic leaves around the flower.

Spray a 30cm (12in) length of thin wood dowel gold and bind with narrow giftwrap ribbon. Glue the ends in place. Pull two lengths of giftwrap ribbon between your thumb and finger to coil them. Stick the ribbons to one end of the dowel with sticky tape and use a strong glue to stick the wooden handle behind the mask.

# CLOWNING AROUND

# STRIKE UP THE BAND

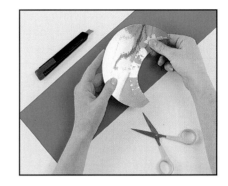

Here's a jaunty majorette's cap that is ideal for a fancy dress party. Cut a strip of coloured cardboard 60cm x 13cm (24in x 5in) Use the template on page 93 to cut out a peak in silver cardboard. On the wrong side, score the peak along the broken lines and make snips in the cardboard to the scored line. Bend the snipped edge upwards.

Stick an 18cm (7 in) long strip of double-sided tape in the middle of one long edge of the hat on the wrong side. Overlap the ends of the strip and lightly hold together with masking tape. Press the snipped edge of the peak onto the sticky tape. Remove the masking tape.

These conical hats are so easy to make that you will want to make one for each of your party guests. Cut a 30cm (12in) diameter circle of shiny cardboard for each hat and cut to the centre. Cut a slice out of the circle so that the hat is not too bulky. Overlap the cut edges and glue together.

Wrap the hat around your head, overlapping the ends, and stick together with double-sided tape. Pleat a rectangle of foil giftwrap and bind the lower edge closed with clear sticky tape, forming a fan. Glue to the front of the hat. Finally, cut out a diamond shape from silver cardboard and glue it over the fan.

There are many ways to decorate the hats – stick on gold stars or use glitter pens to draw a pattern. Another idea is to spread glue in moon shapes on the hat and then sprinkle on glitter, shaking off the excess.

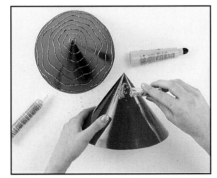

Make a hole with the points of a pair of scissors each side of the hat and thread with hat elastic. Adjust the elastic to fit under the chin and make a knot behind the holes.

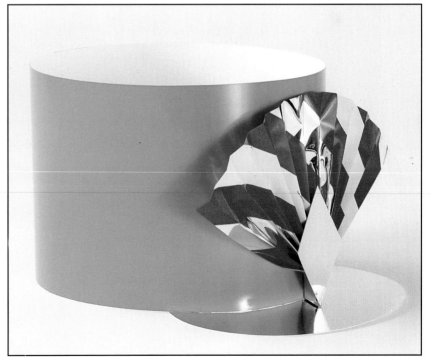

Making your own personalized giftwrap, decorations and gift tags is not only fun, it adds a touch of class to any present. This section shows you how to decorate your own paper and create co-ordinating gift tags and ribbons, rosettes and bows. We also focus on the best ways to wrap presents of an odd shape, or how to disguise familiar shaped gifts such as records. And no Christmas would be complete without the greeting card; so why not show someone you really care by making a card especially for them? There are greeting cards for the whole family to make; you don't even have to make the basic card as most craft shops sell card 'blanks' especially for this purpose.

Stencilling is an easy and effective way to decorate paper. Draw a simple motif on cardboard to use as a template and cut it out. Trace around the motif at random on stencil board.

Use a craft knife and a cutting board to cut out the stencil shapes.
Place the stencil over the paper and hold in place with masking tape.

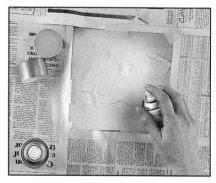

Tape scraps of the stencil board over some of the cut-outs. Spray evenly over the stencil with gold spray paint. When the paint is dry uncover the other stencils and cover the painted ones. Now spray with silver spray paint. Leave to dry.

# FAN TOPPED GIFTBOX

# BRONZE AND SILVER BOUQUET

A fan adds panache to a plain giftbox. Cut one long edge from a large rectangular paper doily, making it about 7cm (2 ³/₄in) deep. Cut cartridge paper a little deeper and wider than this and cover with foil gift wrap using spray adhesive. Glue the doily strip to one side. Cut the top edge following the curves of the doily, then pleat up concertina style.

Open out the concertina into a fan shape and run a length of double-sided tape along the base to hold it in place. Do not remove the backing paper. From narrow curling ribbon cut five 15cm (6in) lengths, and from foil, five 6cm (2¹/₂in) squares. Stick a square to the end of each ribbon with double-sided tape and curl the foil around it. Secure the end with more tape.

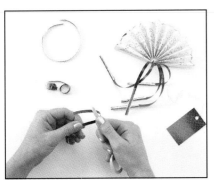

Remove the backing paper from the base of the fan and stick the ribbon ends to the centre. Make a gift tag from a rectangle of paper and cover with foil using spray adhesive. Punch a hole in it, attach a length of gold thread and join to the fan. Curl the ends of three lengths of ribbon and stick them to the front of the fan with PVA glue or tape. Stick the fan diagonally across the giftbox.

Paint-sprayed plastic holly adds a flourish to a plain box. Spray two sprigs of holly with silver then, when dry, spray lightly with bronze to highlight the leaves and berries. Wire the holly together, then wire on three small glass balls, chosen to colour match the gift wrap. Wrap a piece of double-sided tape around the stems and wrap with silver crepe paper, gluing the end down.

To make the bow, cut a strip of silver crepe paper along the length of the roll, 74cm (29in) long and 12.5 (5in) wide. Fold in the two long edges to overlap and crimp the folded edges between your fingers, gently stretching the paper. Pinch into a bow shape and wrap a short length of crepe paper, raw edges tucked in, around the centre. Secure with double-sided tape.

Cut a 6.5cm (2¹/₂in) wide strip of crepe paper along the length of the roll as before, cutting enough to wrap around the giftbox in both directions. Crimp the edges and attach to the box with double-sided tape, placing the joins under the box. Press a double-sided adhesive pad to the centre cross of the ties and press the holly bouquet in place. Finally, stick the bow in place over the holly.

# GIFT BOX ROSETTE

# TISSUE TWISTS

You will need the type of gift wrap ribbon which sticks to itself when moistened for this decoration. First cut two strips of ribbon at least 40cm (16in) long. Twist each piece into a figure-of-eight, moistening the ends to hold in place. Stick one piece at right angles over the other. Repeat with two more strips 5cm (2in) shorter.

Stick the second rosette on top of the first. To finish, make a loop out of a short strip of ribbon and stick it in the centre. For a more traditional rosette, simply make the loops shorter and tighter.

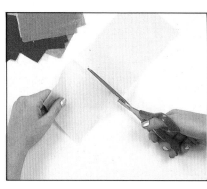

You can make these decorations in a single colour, but they look more effective if you choose several. For each twist, you need three squares of tissue for the outer colour, two for the middle colour and two for the inner (most visible) section. The squares needed for the inner section are smaller than those for the outside; the middle leaves must be of a size in between.

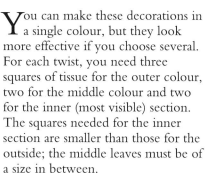

Pick up the squares in order, putting one on top of the other; outer colour first, then the middle, then the inner squares. Position them so that the corners of each square are at a different angle, as shown. Put a couple of stitches through the centre point to secure all the squares together and leave some thread hanging.

Fold the whole thing in half and half again, twisting the folded point at the base to form the shape of the 'flower'. Pull the thread out at the point, and wind it tightly around the twisted base to secure it; 'fluff' out the finished decoration. Make several 'flowers' and group them together on your present.

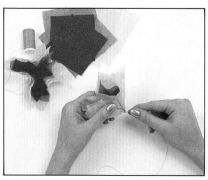

# CHRISTMAS BOXES

# POSIES FOR PRESENTS

A delicate posy of dried flowers provides a perfect decoration for any gift. Choose a selection of brightly coloured, small-headed flowers and tie them together with fine wire. The flowers used here are blue larkspur, yellow South African daisy, (a type of helichrysum), small red roses and a touch of golden rod. Wrap a strip of white ribbon around the stems and finish off with a bow.

The posy on this gift box is made up in a similar way, using flowers in a range of colours that match those of the box. The posy contains green amaranthus (love-lies-bleeding), mauve xeranthemums, pink gypsophila (baby's breath), blue larkspur, cream 'cauliflower' and yellow dudinea.

Attach the posies to the gifts with glue. Alternatively you can wire them on. To do this you will need to pierce two small holes in the side of the box. Wrap wire round the stems of the posy and thread it through the holes; secure on the inside.

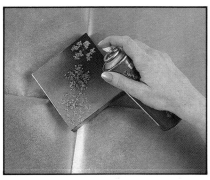

This is a simple but elegant way to use empty gift boxes as containers for pot-pourri. We have selected a green and a black box. Take the lid off one of the boxes and lightly secure three whole flower heads of cow parsley diagonally across it. With aerosol spray paint, give the top of the box two light coats of gold paint.

When the paint is dry, remove the parsley to reveal the unsprayed part of the box. This shows up as a pretty pattern through the paint. Now fix the gold sprayed cow parsley to the other box lid. These boxes are filled with 'Noel' pot-pourri, which is a festive mixture of small cones, tree bark and citrus peel. Cover the pot-pourri with cling film (plastic wrap) before replacing the lids.

# CONCENTRIC CIRCLES

# PAINT AND MATCH

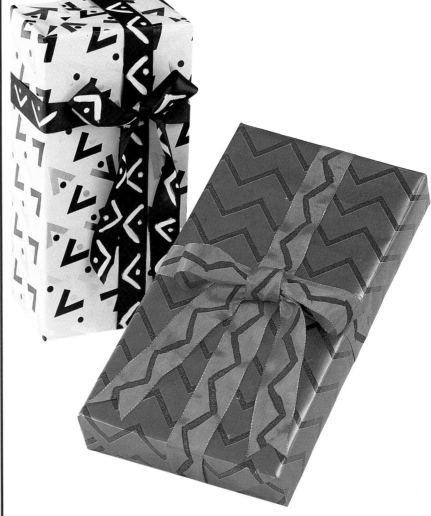

H ow to give a tall thin present even more presence! Take a spool of gift ribbon — the sort that sticks to itself when moistened. Roll a length round your thumb to form a small circle; moisten and stick in position.

Make another ring, larger than the first; stick that down too. Make another circle, and another, ensuring that their increase in size is in the same proportion each time. Four circles is about the maximum the ribbon can take before flopping slightly and thus losing the crispness of the decoration.

I t is quite easy to paint wide ribbon to co-ordinate with your wrapping paper. And the results are stunning! Choose a gift wrap with a simple design. Decide whether you want the ribbon to be a positive version of the paper's design, like the blue example shown here, or a negative one, like the black and white suggestions. Experiment with poster paint on your chosen ribbon.

Keep the design very simple and stylized. When you're happy with your pattern, paint enough ribbon to wrap up the gift, allowing sufficient for a fairly large bow. Leave the ribbon to dry thoroughly before tying it around the parcel. If the paint does crack a little when tying up the ribbon, simply touch it up and leave it to dry again.

# SEQUIN SHEEN

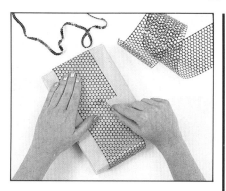

The metallic sheen of sequins, and the strip of metallic plastic from which they are pressed, looks rather chic. Sequin waste — that is, the strip of metallic plastic — can be bought by the metre or yard from good craft shops. This idea looks best on rectangular flat parcels. Wrap a piece of sequin waste around the length of the present; fix it with tape.

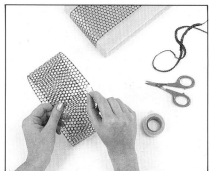

Take another strip of sequin waste and join the two ends to make a large loop. Use sticky tape to fix them, making sure the holes overlap so that the join is almost invisible.

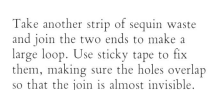

Put a strip of threaded sequin trim of the same colour across the middle of the loop. Remove a few loose sequins so that you can tie the trim in position. Repeat with another length of trim; space the two evenly apart in the centre of the loop to form a bow. Attach the bow to the parcel with double-sided tape. Sequin trim as a gift tie in its own right gives a glamorous finish to any gift.

# LOOPING THE LOOP

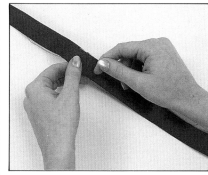

This decoration looks best on a rectangular gift. Take 66cm (26in) of woven ribbon; lay it flat. Measure 13cm (5in) from one end of the ribbon and mark both edges. Then mark along the ribbon's length a further 10cm (4in), 7.5cm (3in), 5cm (2in), 7.5cm (3in), 10cm (4in). Using one piece of thread, pick up tiny stitches at each mark along one edge.

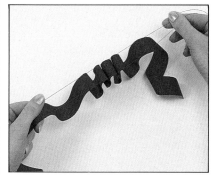

Run a similar gathering thread up the other edge of ribbon, making sure that the stitches are exactly level on both sides. Gather up the loops as shown; it's easiest to knot the two threads together at one end of the gathers and ease the loops along.

Pull the thread tight to make properly-formed loops; sew the joins in place and cut off the excess thread. Tie the ribbon around the gift and use double-sided tape to attach the loops in the centre of the long side of the gift. Snip a diagonal cut at the ends of the ribbon tails.

Here is a novel way to disguise two lightweight presents. Put each gift in a rectangular box and wrap with giftwrap. Apply double-sided tape to the end of one box (the smallest, if they vary in size). Peel off the tape backing and press the gift against the other one making an 'L' shape.

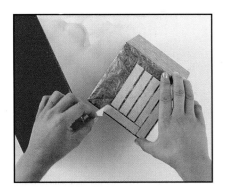

From mounting board, cut two large circles for the back wheels and two smaller ones for the front. Cut a circle for each wheel in giftwrap with 1.5cm (⁵⁄₈in) added all around. Stick the wheel on the wrong side and snip into the edge all around. Apply double-sided tape to the circumference of the wheel and stick the snipped edge over onto the tape.

Cut giftwrap circles slightly smaller than the wheels and stick to the wrong side. Use a craft knife to cut a slice from a cardboard tube for the funnel. Apply double-sided tape in a cross shape over one end and remove the backing tape. Roll the funnel in a strip of giftwrap, snip the excess at the top and tuck it inside.

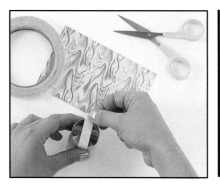

Use a strong glue to stick the wheels to the sides of the train, then press the funnel onto the 'engine'. Stick three lengths of narrow giftwrapping ribbon together at one end. To coil the ribbon, pull the lengths smoothly over the blades of a pair of scissors. Stick the ribbon inside the funnel for the 'smoke'.

Disguise the unmistakable shape of a record by making it look like a cushion. First create paper tassels. Cut a piece of coloured paper into narrow strips leaving about 2.5cm (1in) at the bottom uncut so that you create a fringe. Roll up the fringe, catching in a short length of narrow ribbon. Secure the tassel with coloured tape.

Take some wrapping paper that is more than twice the size of the gift, fold it in half around the record and cut it so that it is just a little larger. Join two of the sides together with coloured tape along their full length, attaching the ends of the tassels at the corners as you do so. Put a strip of tape over the folded edge of the 'bag'.

Stuff the inside of the 'bag' on both sides of the record with shredded tissue, being careful to put some in the corners. Don't use too much or the wrapping paper will wrinkle. Seal along the remaining open edge with tape.

For an extra special gift at Christmas, wrap your present to look like a prayer book. Wrap the gift in gold paper so that it will look like the closed pages of the book. The last flap should not be folded in the usual way, but should be cut precisely to fit the side of the gift as shown; glue it in place.

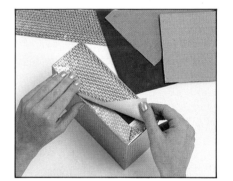

Take two pieces of thick cardboard slightly larger than the size of the gift. You will also need a long strip of thin cardboard measuring the width and length of the gift. Use tape to stick the thick cardboard on to either side of the thin cardboard to make a book cover for the gift. Cover the outside with plain paper as shown; glue all the edges down firmly.

Spread glue over the inside of the book cover, and place the gift firmly on one side of it. Wrap the cover over the other side of the gift, making sure it's stuck properly. Cut out gold crosses (or other appropriate symbols relevant for your recipient's religion) and stick them in place.

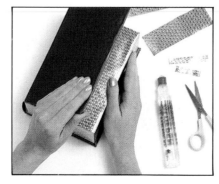

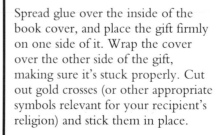

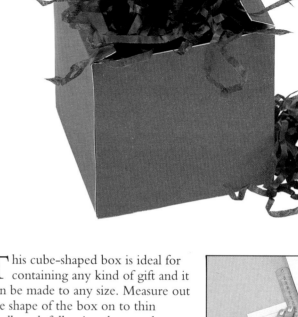

Making a box from scratch can be a little complicated, so why not start with an empty cereal packet? Take your cereal packet and carefully open it out flat. Separating the joins needs care - if necessary slide a knife between the seams to part the glue, rather than tear the packet.

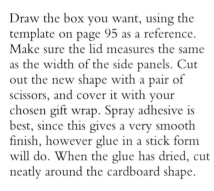

Draw the box you want, using the template on page 95 as a reference. Make sure the lid measures the same as the width of the side panels. Cut out the new shape with a pair of scissors, and cover it with your chosen gift wrap. Spray adhesive is best, since this gives a very smooth finish, however glue in a stick form will do. When the glue has dried, cut neatly around the cardboard shape.

Score along the new fold lines of the box using the back of a craft knife or the blunt edge of a pair of scissors. Fold the box into shape. Stick the side flap in place as shown; you can use double-sided tape or glue. Fix the two flaps on the bottom (either glue them or tape them). Put in some shredded tissue as padding, slot in your gift and tuck the lid neatly in place.

This cube-shaped box is ideal for containing any kind of gift and it can be made to any size. Measure out the shape of the box on to thin cardboard, following the template on page 95. It's very important that all the squares are exactly the same size and that all the angles are right angles. Cut out the shape, and score along the fold lines - the back of a craft knife is useful for doing this.

Bend the card carefully along the score lines, making a neat crease along each fold. Crease the flaps on the lid and base and fold the four sides into the shape of the box.

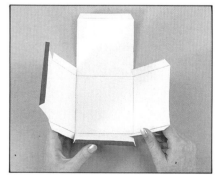

Stick the side flap to its opposite side as shown. You can glue this, or alternatively, use double-sided tape. Fold in the base flap - it should fit precisely and thus give the box rigidity. Finally, close the lid flap.

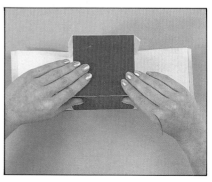

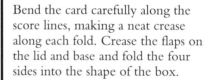

# PUT A LID ON IT

# IT'S A COVER-UP

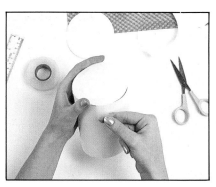

A cylindrical box looks much more difficult to make than it is. Wrap a piece of thin cardboard around the gift to determine the measurement of the box. Cut out the cardboard, roll it up and stick down the edge with a length of tape. Draw and cut out a circular base, and a slightly larger circle for the lid. Attach the base with small bits of tape.

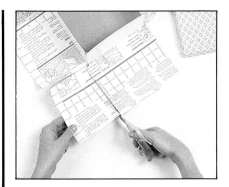

When re-covered in plastic, a shoe box makes a great container for a present. Put the box in the centre of a piece of self-adhesive plastic and draw around it. Then draw around the shape of the sides and ends of the box so you end up with a diagram of the 'exploded' box. Allow extra plastic all round for overlaps. Cut out the pattern you have just created.

Cut a strip of cardboard slightly longer than the circumference of the cylinder. To make the lid, stick the edge of the strip to the edge of the circle with tape. Next, spread glue on some gift wrap and roll the cylinder in it. Cut the paper to fit, allowing an overlap each end. Tuck the overlap into the open end; secure. Fold the base overlap in a series of small triangles and stick to the base.

Peel the backing off the plastic and position the box carefully in the middle of the covering. Smooth the rest of the plastic up over the box, starting with the ends. Wrap the small overlap around the corners as shown.

Draw a circle of gift wrap slightly smaller than the base. Cut it out and glue in position, hiding all the folds and bits of tape. Cover the lid in the same way. If you like, you can punch two holes in each side of the container and thread through short lengths of decorative braid.

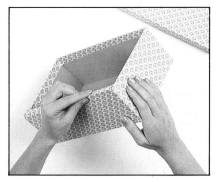

Smooth the plastic up over the sides, trimming off the edges to make the pieces the exact size of the sides. Fold over the overlaps around the rim. Cover the lid in the same way. For complete co-ordination, you could cover the inside of the box to match. Alternatively, you could line the box with co-ordinating tissue paper or net.

Cut a gold card 30cm x 15cm (12in x 6in) and score 7.5cm (3in) in from each side. Trace off the template on page 95 and carefully work out where the points will fall. Mark the design on the back of the gold card and cut out using a sharp craft knife and ruler for straight edges.

Burnish the edges of the gold card with the back of your thumb nail if they have lifted. Cut king's clothes from three pieces of brocade, slightly larger than the apertures. Place small pieces of double-sided tape around the kings on the inside of the card and stick brocade in place.

Cut the kings' gifts from gold card and glue in place. Attach sequins to the points of their crowns. Stick on a piece of white card to cover the back of the centre panel. To protect the points, slip a further piece of card into the envelope. The three kings which have been cut out could be used for a further card or gift tag.

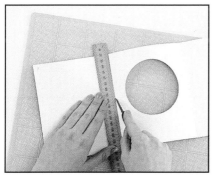

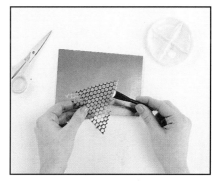

N̲ew Year celebrations are particularly associated with Scotland. So here, in traditional Scottish style, we have tartan and golden bells for our New Year greeting. A ready-cut window card was used. Remove the left-hand section off a 3-fold card with a sharp craft knife and ruler. Use this spare card to make two bells.

C̲ut a card 15cm x 22cm (6in x 8½in), score and fold in half widthways. Mark the centre top of the card with a pencil dot. Cut a triangle from sequin waste and stick centrally on the card applying a little glue around the edges only. Hold in place on the card until the glue dries. Any residue glue can be rubbed away afterwards.

Cut a piece of tartan fabric or paper to fit inside the back of the card, attach with spray glue and trim the edges. Draw two bell shapes onto the spare gold card. Cut out and back with tartan using spray glue. Trim with small scissors and punch holes in the top.

Cut a base for the tree from a piece of cardboard or paper. Curl over scissors a number of pieces of narrow gift wrap ribbon, cut about 9.5cm (3¾in) long.

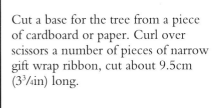

Make a bow from narrow satin ribbon and cut a length of ribbon for the bells to hang from. Thread the first bell and hold in place with a dab of glue, then thread the second bell. Sew the bow onto the card, above the aperture, and through the ribbon suspending the bells.

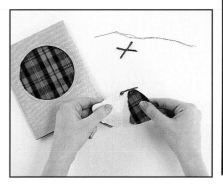

Glue on the base and add a sequin star to the top of the tree. Slip the curled ribbons through every other hole in the sequin waste and every other row, starting at the top of the tree. You shouldn't have to glue them as they will stay in place. But you will need to deliver this card by hand if it is not to get squashed.

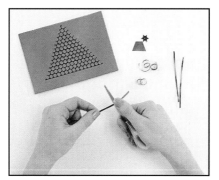

# CANDLELIT CHRISTMAS TREE

# CATHEDRAL WINDOWS

Cut a green card 15cm x 20cm (6in x 8in) and score down the centre. Draw one half of a Christmas tree and cut out a paper template. Draw around this onto the green card, reversing the template along the scored line; cut out. Set your sewing machine to a wide satin stitch and, moving the card from side to side, sew the garlands. Pull loose threads through to the back and knot.

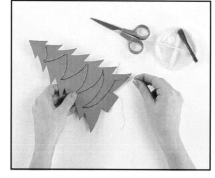

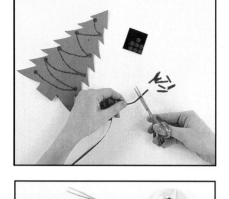

Decorate the tree with self-adhesive spots to resemble Christmas tree baubles. Then cut narrow satin ribbon into fourteen 1cm (½in) strips.

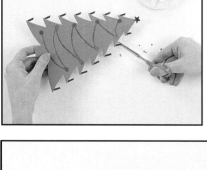

Glue strips in place at the end of the branches on the back of the card: tweezers will help you to hold them steady. Leave until the glue dries, then cut the tops diagonally to look like candles. Add the finishing touch with a red star on top of the tree.

On red fabric, draw four 9cm (3½in) squares and cut them out. Fold in a 6mm (¼in) seam allowances and press. Find the centre of each square by folding it diagonally twice and press with the tip of an iron. Open out the squares, then fold the corners into the centre. Catch the centre points with a small stitch. Fold in again and sew along the seams!

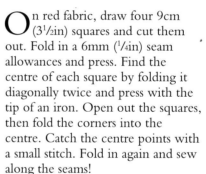

Cut four 2cm (¾in) squares from fir-tree fabric. Place two red squares right sides together and sew down one side to make a double square. Pin a fir-tree patch diagonally over the seam on the right side, and curl back the red folds surrounding the patch to cover the raw edges. Slip stitch to hold in place. Repeat to make another double square.

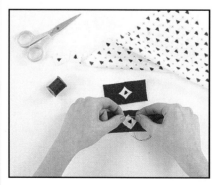

Sew the double squares together and place a third and fourth fir-tree patch over the seams. Sew tiny beads in the corners. Cut a card 25cm x 18cm (10in x 7in), score and fold in half. Mark the top centre and 6cm (2½in) down either side. Cut out to form a point. Glue the finished square onto the card and draw a border with a gold felt-tip pen.

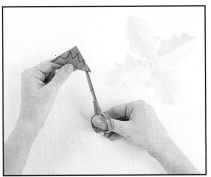

C ut a silver card 30cm x 15cm (12in x 6in), score and fold in half widthways. Trace the holly templates from page 95 and transfer onto thin cardboard. Cut a 13cm (5in) square of green satin paper and a 10cm (4in) square of dark green tissue-paper. Fold both squares in half twice, then diagonally to make a triangle.

Cut out the larger holly from satin paper and unfold, then the smaller holly in dark green paper. Hold the holly templates in place on the paper triangles with paper clips when cutting out. Or you can draw around the templates first if you find it easier.

Spray glue onto the backs of the holly leaves. Position the larger, pale green leaves first, then the dark green on top, between the pale green leaves. Add five or so red berries using self-adhesive spots.

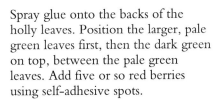

A dd a musical note to your greetings this Christmas. The treble clefs are buttons. Cut a glossy red card 22cm x 15cm (8½in x 6in). Score and fold in half widthways. Draw a square 5.5cm x 7.5cm (2¼in x 3in) on white paper. Rule two staves – groups of five lines 3mm (⅛in) apart – using a fine black felt-tipped pen. Cut out the square.

Centre the square of music paper on the card so that you have an equal margin on three sides. Visually, it is better to have a larger margin at the base of the card. Mark the corners of the music sheet lightly on the card and stick down using spray glue. Place the opened card on a piece of felt and pierce two holes for the two buttons using dividers or a thick needle.

From the back, sew on the buttons through the holes you have pierced, then knot the thread and trim. Finish the knots with a dab of glue.

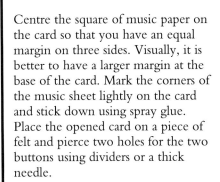

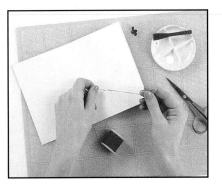

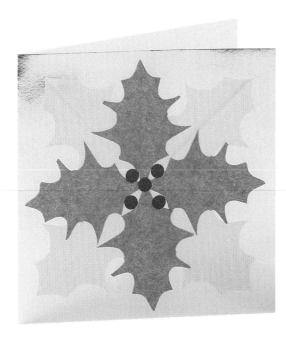

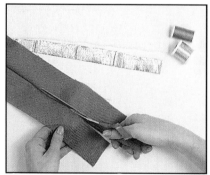

To make these quick festive cards, we purchased some ready-cut 3 fold cards, and used stickers and buttons to decorate them. Cut three strips of fabric in suitable colours: here blue glitter-spotted material has been used for the sky, silver lamé for the frozen landscape and white towelling for the snow.

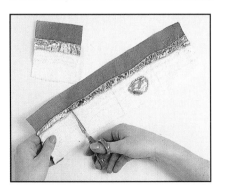

Machine the strips together with a wide satin stitch, machining over twice if you want a thicker line. Measure the size of the card's aperture and mark cutting lines on the fabric. Machine trees with lines of stitches, or cut circles of lamé and make ponds. Use your imagination to dream up a different idea for each card.

Cut out the sections and sew buttons in place or attach stickers. Using double-sided tape, mount the pieces over the back of the apertures and glue the extra flap down on each card. Extra sequins can be added to the borders for the moon or stars.

A dove of peace for New Year. It is made from a paper doiley with calendar dates falling from its beak. Cut a deep blue card 30cm x 20cm (12in x 8in), score and fold in half. Draw freehand two curves at the top of the front of the card to represent clouds and cut with a craft knife.

Trace the dove pattern from page 95 and transfer to thin cardboard to make your own template. Trace out a dove onto a white paper doiley and cut out, together with the dates one and 31 from an old calendar. Also cut a strip of translucent film, making it wavy along the upper edge to resemble hills.

Make a template from the pattern on page 95 and cut an extra template for the wing (see finished card). Draw round the dove twice on dark blue felt so that the birds face opposite directions. Cut them out. Cut two pieces of muslin 18cm x 11.5cm (7in x 4½in), position the doves between both layers and pin. Tack the layers together to hold the doves in place.

Spray glue all the pieces and place on the card together with four star sequins. Finally, using a felt-tipped silver pen, draw a line along the edge of the cloud curves.

Using two strands of embroidery thread, sew tiny running stitches around the doves and stitch the feet (see finished card). Place the wing template over the doves and lightly draw around them with a sharp pencil. Quilt along these lines. When finished, take out the tacking thread and lightly press.

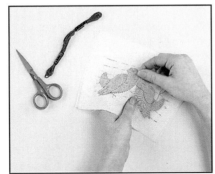

Purchase a 3-fold window card to fit the quilted doves. Cut out a matching window from the left-hand section of the card. Trim the muslin to about 6mm (¼in) larger than the window. Stick the quilt down using double-sided tape. Add tiny round beads for the doves' eyes and pearl beads to the corners of the window.

M̲ake a traditional Christmas card from pressed ferns. Cut a rectangle of white cardboard 16.5cm x 6.5cm (6½in x 2½in). Select a piece of bracken about 14cm (5½in) in length. Fix the bracken to the card with spots of glue. Leave sufficient space at the base of this 'tree' for the 'flower pot'. For the star, spray a floret of fools' parsley gold, and glue to the top of the tree.

From red metallic board cut a rectangle 21.5cm x 20cm (8½in x 8in); crease, and fold in half lengthways. Now draw a rectangle - larger than the white card using a gold marker. Cut out a 'flower pot' from some red board, draw on some decorative lines and fix the pot to the tree. Cover the design card with protective film and fix it centrally within the gold border.

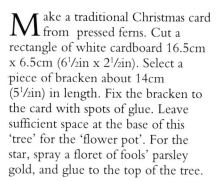

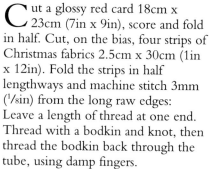

C̲ut a glossy red card 18cm x 23cm (7in x 9in), score and fold in half. Cut, on the bias, four strips of Christmas fabrics 2.5cm x 30cm (1in x 12in). Fold the strips in half lengthways and machine stitch 3mm (⅛in) from the long raw edges: Leave a length of thread at one end. Thread with a bodkin and knot, then thread the bodkin back through the tube, using damp fingers.

Thread a length of double wool through each tube. Pin the ends of the tubes to a firm surface. To plait them, lay all four strands over the left hand, then take the left strand over the two middle strands and the right strand over one. Continue in this way to the end. Ease into a circle, cross over the ends and sew through to secure. Trim and finish with a bow.

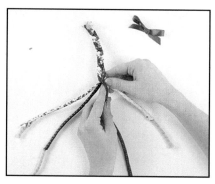

Bind the trimmed ends with embroidery cotton. Draw an arched border onto the card using a gold pen. Centre the finished wreath and pierce through the card with a thick needle. Sew through from the back of the card to hold the garland in place. Knot the thread, trim and finish with a dot of glue to hold firm.

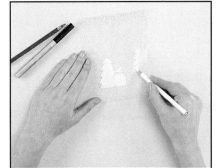

A simple, easily-made card in unusual colours for Christmas. Cut a card 11cm x 20cm (4¼in x 8in), score and fold in half. Keep the fold at the top of the card. Cut a strip of green plastic from an old shopping bag. Tear four strips of tissue in shades of orange and yellow. The fir-tree is taken from a strip of self-adhesive stickers.

A friendly snowman invites you to come outside to play. Cut off the left-hand side of a 3-fold card so that light will shine through the window. Cut a piece of film slightly smaller than the folded card. Draw a snowman and trees on to paper to fit between the window bars. Place the paper under the film and trace the outline of the snowman and trees with a silver pen.

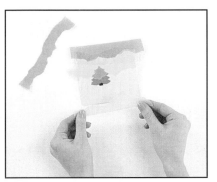

Arrange the strips so that the colours overlap and produce new colours and tones. Stick the tree in place, then spray glue onto the backs of the strips and stick down also.

Turn the film over and colour in the trees and the snowman using a white chinagraph pencil.

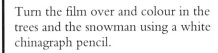

Trim any excess paper from the edges of the card with a sharp craft knife and steel ruler.

Turn the film the right way up and draw a scarf and nose with a red chinagraph pencil. Add face details in silver. Attach the film to the inside of the card with double-sided tape and place a silver star where it can be seen shining through the window.

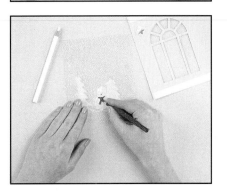

here is a surprise for the person who opens this card. Cut a rectangle of blue cardboard 20cm x 16cm (8in x 6¼in). Score widthwise across the centre and fold in half. Tear white paper into strips and glue across the lower edge on the front and inside. Cut out two green trees from thin cardboard and glue to the front.

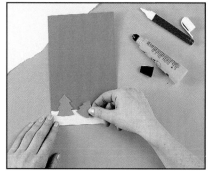

Paint snowflakes with a white typing correction pen. Use the template on page 94 to cut out the snowman in white cardboard, the hat and scarf in yellow and the eyes, nose and buttons in black. Draw a pattern on the scarf and hat with a red pen. Glue all the pieces to the snowman and draw a smile with a black felt-tipped pen.

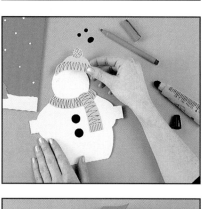

Score along the centre of the snowman and the broken lines on the tabs. Bend the snowman in half along the scored centre and place him inside the card matching the fold to the opening edges of the card and keeping the lower edges level. Glue the tabs inside the card.

Cut a card 18cm x 23cm (7in x 9in). Score and fold in half. Draw a border in silver pen around the card. Make a sock-shaped template out of thin cardboard and draw around it onto red felt using a water-soluble pen. Now hold the template in place over some sequin waste and cut around it.

Sew the sequin waste to the felt by hand or machine, then trim both layers neatly.

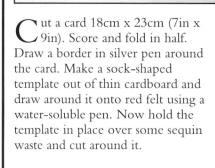
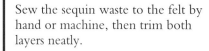

Glue the stocking to the card, then add the little pony eraser or another small gift that can be glued on. Draw holly and berries using felt-tipped pens. You could also add beads and sequins if you wish.

## CHRISTMAS PUFFINS

Colourful puffins, cut from a sheet of wrapping paper, keep a lookout from their perch. Cut a card 28cm x 13cm (18in x 5¼in). The card should be blue on the inside and white on the outside. On the outside, score lines 9cm (3½in) and 19cm (7½in) in from the left and fold. Turn the card over and on the inside score and fold 20cm (8in) in from the left.

Cut out three puffins and spray glue the first one on to the outside of the far right-hand panel of card, facing right. Cut around him with a craft knife leaving him attached to the card by his tail. The score line on the outside will allow him to stand forward.

Glue the other two puffins in place on the inside. Any wrapping paper with a distinct animal motif can be used in this way to make a striking card.

## POLAR BEAR

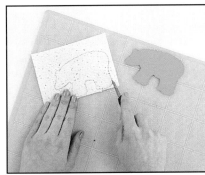

Cut a card 23cm x 18cm (9in x 7in), score and fold in half. Trace the pattern from page 95 and transfer it onto thin cardboard to make a template. Place on some polystyrene wallpaper and draw around it with a soft pencil. Cut out with a craft knife. Also cut out some ice caps and ground from iridescent plastic or silver paper.

Glue down the mountains, ground and polar bear, placing the latter in front of the peaks. Then decorate with silver sequin stars.

With a silver pen draw in the polar bear's features: the legs, paws and ears. As an alternative, the polar bear could also be made from white felt.

# FUN FOLD-OUT

If you have a long message for the recipient of your gift, this fold-out tag allows lots of room. Select a gift wrap design that has a fairly large repeat. One motif must have sufficient space around it so that it can be cut out without including any others. Draw a rectangle around the motif, ensuring that all the corners are right angles.

Cut the rectangle out with a craft knife. Next, cut out a piece of thin cardboard the same height as the chosen motif and exactly three times its width. Fold the cardboard in three widthways, creasing the folds well, then fold the top two sections back on themselves, as shown. Mark the folds in pencil first to be sure they are straight.

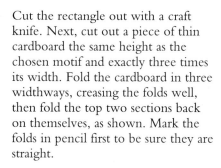

Cut the motif from the gift wrap precisely in half. Glue each half on to the top two sections of the folded card. They should fit exactly, but if necessary trim the top and bottom to form a straight edge. Try matching the colours of the lining cardboard with the gift wrap; in the example shown here, red or even black could have been used, instead of white, for a different effect.

# GIFT BOX TAGS

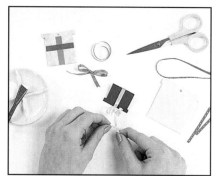

These effective tags are a useful way of using up scraps of cardboard left over from larger projects. Cut a card 10cm x 5cm (4in x 2in), score and fold in half. Measure 6mm (¼in) down from the fold and mark 2mm (⅛in) in from the sides before cutting through both thicknesses with a craft knife to give a 'lid' shape. Run the blade along the steel ruler twice for a clean edge.

Punch a hole through both thicknesses at the centre top. Glue on ribbons in a cross shape, folding the raw edges over to the inside of the tag. Finish off with a bow or curled gift wrap ribbon tied through the hole at the top. The tags can be made up in any size or colour with contrasting ribbons to match your gift.

**M**atch the label to the paper by creating a larger version of a shape which appears in the gift wrap. Begin by drawing a scaled-up shape of the motif from the paper and use it as a template from which to trace the design onto coloured cardboard.

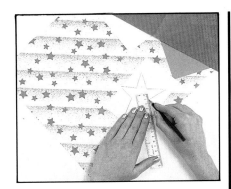

For this idea to be really effective, the colour of the tag should be as close as possible to that in the gift wrap. A layer of tissue laid over cardboard of a near-match, as shown, might make all the difference to duplicating the final colour. Cut out the shape, and punch a hole to enable you to tie it to the gift.

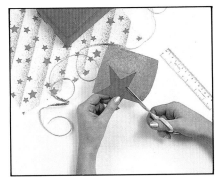

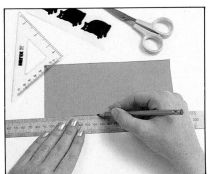

**T**here is such a variety of stickers on the market that you're sure to find one which will make an ideal label for your gift. Take a piece of thin coloured cardboard; this will form the background for the sticker. Draw a rectangle on to the cardboard, twice the width you wish the finished tag to be.

Cut out the rectangle with a craft knife and score down the centre to form the fold; crease well. Remove the sticker from its backing and place it in position on the front of the tag. Punch a hole in the back 'page' of the tag near the fold. Write your message inside and hang the tag on the gift.

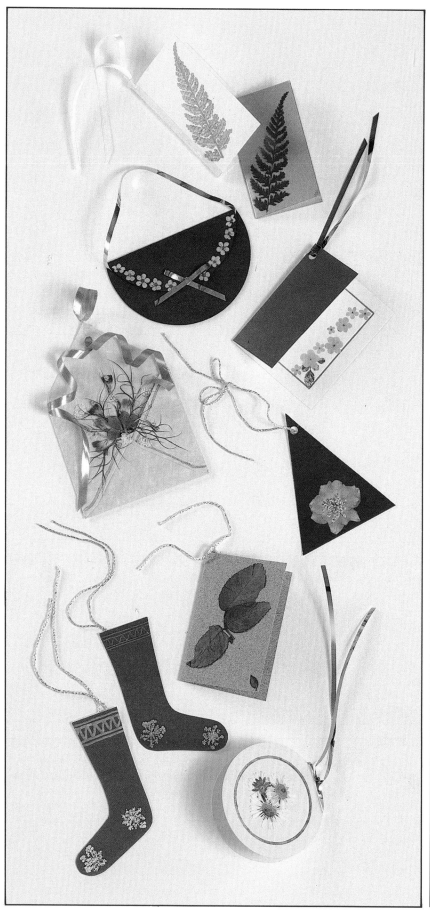

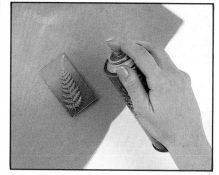

Press some flowers and foliage to make these pretty gift tags. Cut a piece each of red metallic and glossy white cardboard 7.5cm x 10cm (3in x 4in) and fold widthways. Secure a tip of fern to the front of the red card. Spray with gold paint and when dry, lift off the fern, leaving a red silhouette. Fix the gold fern to the front of the white card. Punch a hole and thread with ribbon.

Cut a piece of single-sided glossy green cardboard 7.5cm x 10cm (3in x 4in). Crease and fold 4cm (1½in) from the left edge to give a folded card size of 7.5cm x 6cm (3in x 2½in). With a green marker pen, draw a border inside the larger page. Fix a spray of miniature rose leaves in one corner then form a loose line of guelder rose flowers up the page.

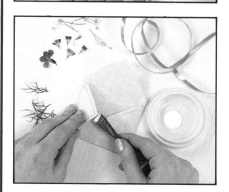

Having looked at the construction of an envelope make a miniature version from a 14cm (5½in) square of paper. Glue the envelope together and line the side flaps with a silver marker. Take wispy foliage, gypsophila and mauve lobelia and secure them inside the envelope so that they appear to be bursting out. Attach some curled mauve ribbon to the top of the tag.

Take some red and green single-sided cardboard and cut out some sock shapes. Using gold or silver aerosol paint, spray heads of fools' parsley; when dry, secure the best shaped florets to the heels and toes of the socks. Draw a ribbed border at the top of each sock, punch a small hole in the corner, and add coloured ties.

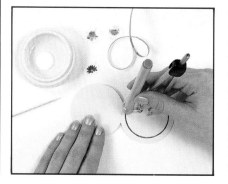

Crease and fold a small piece of yellow cardboard in half and, with your compass pencil just overlapping the fold, draw a 6.5cm (2½in) circle. Cut this out, leaving the card hinged together by about 3cm (1¼in) at the top. Draw a 5cm (2in) circle in green marker pen on the front cover and fix three daisies in the middle. Refold the card and fix a length of thin green ribbon about the fold.

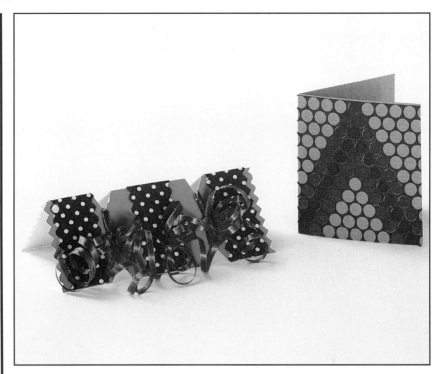

Cut out tags in coloured cardboard or speckled paper. Either cut a single tag and write the message on the back or fold the card in half and cut out a double tag where the message will be inside. Cut a section from a gold paper doily and stick it to the front with spray glue. Trim away any excess level with the edges of the tag.

Pierce a hole on a corner of the tag with the points of a pair of scissors. Cut a length of fine gold cord and bend it in half. Insert the ends through the hole and pull through the loop. Knot the cord ends together or sew them to small gold tassels for extra style.

To decorate the tags further you can write the recipient's name in gold pen and glue on a bow.

To make this dotty Christmas tag, make a cracker-shaped template and trace around it onto brightly coloured cardboard. Reverse the template along one long edge and trace around it again. Cut out the tag and fold it in half. Use pinking shears to trim the ends. Cut three strips of florists' ribbon to fit across the cracker. Pink the edges and spray glue them to the cracker.

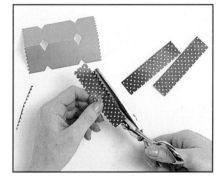

Tie two pieces of giftwrap ribbon around 'ends' of the cracker as shown. Split the ribbon down the centre and curl each length against a scissor blade.

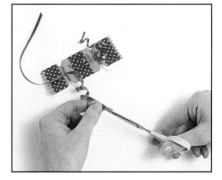

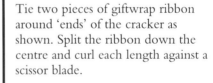

Cut a card 15cm x 7.5cm (6in x 3in), score and fold in half. Cut a piece of sequin waste to fit and attach to the front of the card with spray glue. Colour in circles with felt-tipped pens, many different patterns can be made. Punch a hole in back and thread with ribbon.

In this section, we demonstrate that a hand-made gift can look both stylish and professional, and be a delight to the recipient. Floral gifts are ideal for female friends and relatives; we have selected a range of ideas to choose from, from pot-pourri bags and picture frames to attractive floral arrangements. For the men in your life, there are desk sets, stationery, photograph frames and modern decorative ornaments, such as the ducks on page 82. We've also included soft toys for the children – or your big sister! – and a number of items which you can enhance by painting: plates, pots and china as well as tea cosies and potato print cushions.

These tiny pot-pourri bags are so easy to create, and they make delightful gifts. Take a length of cotton fabric and, using a plate as a pattern, cut out a circle about 25-30cm (10-12in) in diameter. Hem the edge with running stitch, leaving long tails of thread at either end. Cup the fabric circle in your hand as shown and fill it with pot-pourri.

Gather the fabric into a tight ball by pulling the threads. Secure with a knot. Wire together a small tight bunch of helichrysum (strawflower or everlasting) using fine silver rose wire and attach the posy to the bag, threading the wire through the fabric on both sides to secure. (Use a needle to make holes in the fabric first if necessary.)

Make a double bow out of satin ribbon and wire this on to the bag. finally, cut a length of gold cord about 35cm (15in) long and tie it round the posy, finishing with a double knot. Tie the ends of the cords at the desired length and hang the bag by this loop.

# FLORAL PICTURE

# RICH AND RARE

Combine an antique pot with dried flowers for the perfect gift. Note how the blue and orange in the china have been picked up by the colours of the flowers. First, cut a block of florists' foam to fit snugly inside the pot.

Using wired bunches of helichrysum (strawflower or everlasting), build up a dome shape to reflect the shape of the pot. Then add clusters of blue-dyed *Leucodendron brunia*. The unusual bobbly shape of this plant will always add interest to any arrangement.

Finally, add clumps of bright yellow morrison to fill in any gaps and complete the display.

In this attractive design, dried flowers have been used to form a picture. Take a small oval frame and remove the glass, leaving only the backing board. Cut the heads off a colourful selection of plants and start to glue them on to the board. Begin with a red rose in the middle, surrounded by bright yellow yarrow. Add red celosia cockscomb next.

Continue to arrange the heads in small groups, covering the entire surface. The other plants used here are love-in-a-mist heads inside bells of Ireland, lotus seedheads and silver bobbles of *Leucodendron brunia*. The picture is completed with some pearl achillea (a type of yarrow) dotted in amongst the *Leucodendron*.

# ALL AROUND MY HAT

# NEPTUNE'S GOLD

A small straw hat, decorated with a garland of dried flowers, makes a pretty gift. This particular hat is a small doll's hat. Begin by making three double bows out of satin ribbon. Tie a second length of ribbon round the middle of one of the bows to form the long 'tails' at the back of the hat.

Make a garland to wrap around the crown as follows. Attach some rose wire to a length of string, about 20-25cm (8-10in) from one end. Place a small bunch of flowers over the join and secure with the wire. Add another bunch to cover the stems of the first and bind as before. Continue adding to the garland in this way until it is the desired length.

The flowers used in this garland are red amaranthus (love-lies-bleeding), south African daisy (helichrysum) and golden dyandra. Wrap the garland round the crown and tie the ends of the string together to secure. Wire a couple of bows to the front of the hat and put the other one over the join at the back.

Three clam shells provide the perfect setting for a colourful miniature arrangement. First you must carefully bore a hole in the base of each shell using a braddle. Now fix the shells together with wire, fanning two of them out as shown and using the third as a base. Slice a section off a sphere of florists' foam and cut it to fit the base of the shells. Glue the foam in position.

Cut off a number of honesty (silver dollar plant) seedheads and insert them singly into the foam, covering it completely. Next add small wired bunches of tiny red roses, concentrating them in the middle. Follow with clumps of golden quaking grass, positioning them so that they fan out from the centre of the arrangement and form a star-shaped outline.

Fill in amongst the quaking grass with clumps of bright yellow cluster-flowered helichrysum (strawflower or everlasting), packing them tightly into the arrangement.

## BRASS SHELL

## LATE SUMMER ROSES

$I$n this attractive arrangement, peachy coloured dried flowers set off a small brass trinket box to perfection. Cut a section from a cylinder of florists' foam to fit inside the box and secure with a strip of florists' tape.

Build up the shape of the display with cluster-flowered sunray and a few strands of creamy nipplewort (or broom bloom). The latter will add a fluffy softness to the arrangement.

Next add the focal flowers which are peachy South African daisies (a type of helichrysum). Wire them in small groups and intersperse them throughout. Finish off with a few cones to add an interesting contrast of colour and texture.

$A$ jet black wooden box provides a frame for this pretty dried flower arrangement, and helps to bring out the subtle warmth of the roses. Cut a block of florists' foam to fit the box and wedge it tightly in place. If the fit is good there should be no need to tape it.

Build up the outline using wired bunches of white bupleurum. Keep the shape well within that of the box. Start to fill in the outline with South African daisies (a type of helichrysum), using them to cover the foam. Make the flowers shorter at the front of the display, slightly overhanging the edge of the box.

Complete the picture with several rust-coloured roses, recessing some deep into the arrangement. Gently pull back the outer petals if necessary to open out the flowers before you position them.

## FLOWER SIEVE

This imaginative gift is ideal for displaying in a kitchen. Cut a sphere of florists' foam in two and tape one half on the side of an old flour sieve. Build up a spiky outline using ears of wheat, pushing them singly into the foam. Keep the arrangement asymmetrical by making the stems longer on one side so that they spill out of the bottom of the 'frame'.

Follow the general outline already created using pink larkspur, keeping it as tall as the wheat. Intersperse the arrangement with South African daisies (a type of helichrysum). Place them at varying heights, then add depth with several bunches of moon grass, pushing them well into the display.

Complete the picture with a small posy on top of the sieve; wire together a small group of plants, then cover the wire with raffia. Finish off with a bow and glue the posy on to the sieve.

## THE BELLS ARE RINGING

A host of tiny dried flowers and grasses cluster round an old but gleaming brass bell, creating a very pretty effect. Cut a slice from a cylinder of florists' foam then cut the slice in half. Gouge out the centre of the two halves and affix the pieces to the handle as shown, using tape.

Build up the shape of the arrangement using single stems of mauve xeranthemum. Position those at the top of the display upright, and those lower down dangling over the bell. Now intersperse with wired clumps of quaking grass, following the same outline. Finish off with bunches of lady's mantle, pushed well into the arrangement.

A couple of old wooden spoons form the basis of a pretty arrangement that would brighten up any kitchen. First, wire the spoons together at an angle as shown, winding the wire round the handles several times to secure firmly.

Wire together several small groups of plants, choosing an attractive range of colours. Shown here is yellow quaking grass, white helichrysum (strawflower or everlasting) and dudinea seedheads. Wire the small groups together to form one large bunch and attach this to the spoons so that the blooms sit prettily over the bowls.

Make a large bright double bow out of satin ribbon and tie it with a second length of ribbon around the spoons and the posy.

A pair of butter pats makes an unusual setting for this kitchen design. Take a length of ribbon and wire up one end. Thread the ribbon through both holes from the front, leaving a long tail between the pats. Loop the ribbon over the top and thread through from the front again, pulling it tight. Make a second loop in the same way, leaving it long for hanging the display.

Secure the wired end of ribbon at the back with a knot; cut off any excess. Wire a small bow on to the front of the pats. Then attach half a sphere of florists' foam to the ribbon 'tail' using tape. Wire small bunches of blue jasilda and tiny red helichrysum and push them into the ball, packing them tightly together.

Add longer stems of blue larkspur, leaving some pieces trailing down the pats to break up the outline of the ball. Finally, wire up short double loops of ribbon and intersperse them among the flowers, finishing off with a couple of longer strands at the bottom.

Pressed flower specimens hung on a ruby satin bow make the perfect gift. Take 2½m (2¾yd) of 7.5cm (3in) wide ribbon, and cut it into three lengths: 50cm (20in), 58cm (23in), and 1.42m (56in). Fold the shortest length, ends to centre, to form a bow and gather the centre using needle and thread. Do the same with the next longest length.

Place the smaller bow on top of the larger one, gather them tightly at the centre, and stitch together. Fold the longest length approximately in half around the centre of the double bow, and sew together at the back to form the knot of the finished bow. Also sew in a small curtain ring at the back by which to hang the design. Trim the ends of the ribbon as shown.

Cut three ovals from beige cartridge paper to fit some miniature plaques. Using a fine pen, write the botanical names of your specimens neatly at the bottom of the ovals. For the first oval, arrange stems, foliage and flowers of forget-me-not to simulate a growing plant. When satisfied with their positioning, fix down with latex adhesive and re-assemble the plaque.

For the second oval, take a large heart's ease and fix it one third of the way up from the base, then add further flowers finishing with the smallest at the top. Now introduce heart's ease leaves to give the appearance of a vigorous young plant. When satisfied, fix in position and then carefully assemble within the plaque.

Place a curved stem in the centre of the third oval and fix borage flowers and buds along the stem in a natural way so that it resembles the top of a growing stem. As before, when you have completed the picture, assemble the plaque. Take the three plaques, and arrange them down the ribbon at regular intervals. Now sew them in place, parting the ribbons slightly.

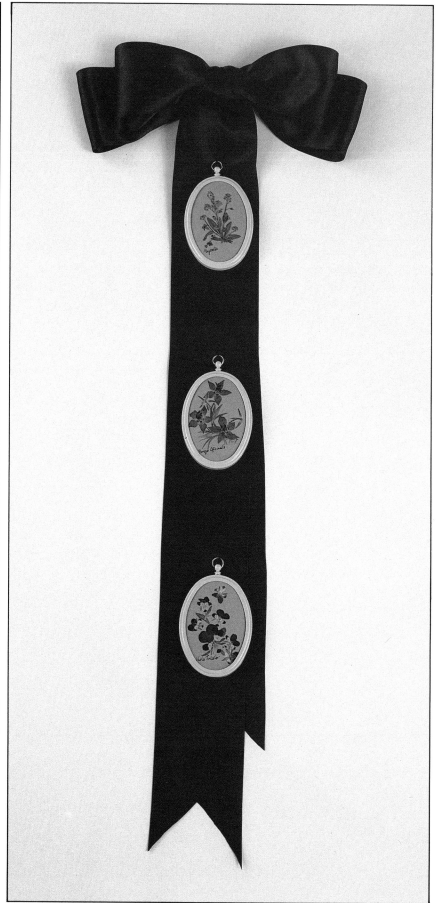

C apture the beauty of a rose in this charming pressed flower design. You will need a round frame 15cm (6cm) in diameter. Cut a mount from coloured paper, then cut a white card to fit the frame. Lay the mount over the white card and lightly pencil in the aperture. Fix single rose leaves in a ring, overlapping, with the tips about 3mm (¹/8in) from the pencilled circle.

Select large rose petals and repeat the process, with the top of the petals overlapping the leaves by 6mm (¹/4in). Both the leaves and petals need to be fixed with very small dabs of latex adhesive. When the glue has dried, carefully rub out the pencil line and blow away the rubbings.

T hese glass drinks coasters - easily available from craft shops - lend themselves to a pressed carnation display and will make a most welcome gift. Cut a circle of moss green cartridge paper to fit into the recess of the large bottle coaster. Now fix large petals of yellow carnation, overlapping them slightly, to form an outer circle.

Fill in the outer circle with smaller carnation petals to create a second circle. Small petals from the centre of the carnation make up the final inner circle. To complete the display fix cow parsley florets to the centre.

Now form an inner circle with smaller petals in the same way. Select the centre part of a rock rose, put a small dot of adhesive right in the middle of the rose ring and, using a palette knife, slide the rock rose into position. Finally, place the mount over the design card, being careful to centre it, and position the cleaned glass over both. Transfer them to the frame and secure the back.

Fit the design card into the recess of the bottle coaster and seal with the circle of baize supplied. Repeat this process for each drinks coaster, using different colours for an attractive display.

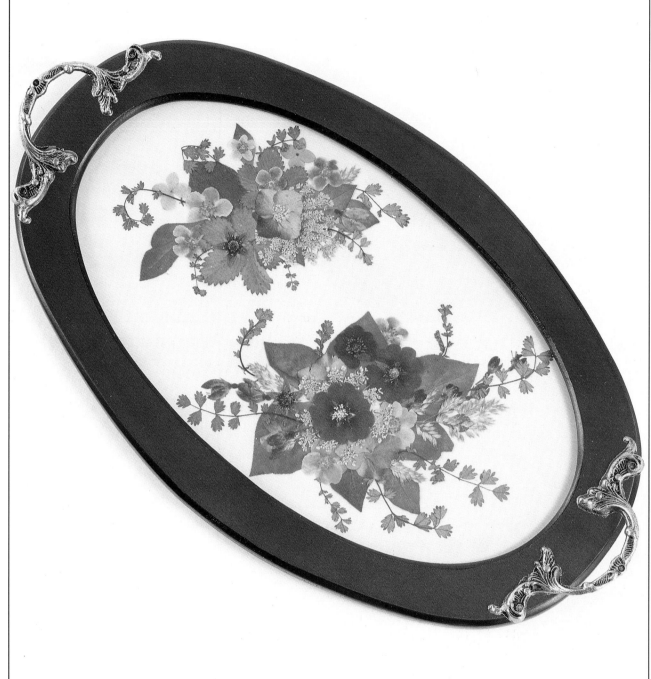

A striking tray, purchased from craft suppliers, makes a perfect setting for this attractive pressed flower design. Fix a cluster of autumn plumbago leaves at one end of the oval card (supplied with the tray) and at the other end fix a smaller cluster of plumbago and autumn wild strawberry leaves. Now enlarge these two clusters with leaf sprays of *Acaena* 'Blue Haze'.

Keep each cluster fairly oval in shape. Working first on the smaller cluster, create a focal point with a red-tinged green hydrangea flower sitting on top of a wild carrot head. Now form a gentle curve of pink potentilla across the top and finish off with green hydrangea and red saxifrage. For the focal point of the larger cluster place a deep red potentilla on top of a head of wild carrot.

To add depth, tuck some pink potentilla and red-tinged hydrangea under the carrot head. Now place two smaller 'Red Ace' potentillas above the focal point. Make a gentle diagonal curve into the centre of the design with buds of Japanese crab apple and finish off with sprays of greyhair grass. Re-assemble the tray according to the manufacturer's instructions.

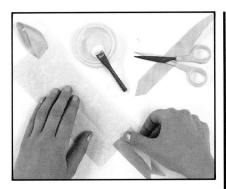

Blue delphiniums and pink candytuft are combined with mauve satin ribbon to create this most attractive pressed flower bookmark. Select a piece of grey imitation parchment paper and cut a rectangle 20cm x 8cm (8in x 3¼in). Crease and fold it in half lengthways. Open up the folded parchment and on the right hand page fix a loop of 2.5cm (1in) wide pale mauve ribbon, using latex adhesive. Cut two pieces of ribbon 9cm (3½in) long and trim in a V-shape. Fix these to the foot of the card as shown. Turn the card over to form the design on the page opposite that bearing the ribbons.

Begin with silverweed leaves facing alternately up the page. Next fix a blue delphinium near the base and overlap with mauve candytuft. Tuck in single candytuft florets under the leaves, gradually decreasing their size up the page and finishing with a few buds. Glue the two pages of card together. Cover both sides with matt protective film (cut to the height of the bookmark and twice the width).

Decorate an enamel canister with pressed flowers for an unusual gift. Secure the canister to your work surface with adhesive putty. Now take a large head of mauve candytuft and fix to the centre of the canister with latex adhesive. Surround the flower with salad burnet leaves and add two more candytuft flowers on either side. Paint over the design with 'two pack' varnish.

For the canister lid, coat with varnish before positioning a circle of salad burnet leaves - slightly apart - around the knob. Fill in between the leaves with large, single candytuft flowers. When dry, seal this design with two thin coats of varnish, feathering the edges with a lint-free cloth.

Give your gift a period touch with this classic decoration. You can use a clear profile sketch or a photograph as a basis for your picture. Make a tracing of the outline and place it face down on the back of a piece of black paper. Redraw the design to transfer it.

Cut out the motif with a pair of small, sharp scissors and glue the design to white paper. Trim the paper to fit your frame. Place the picture in the frame and glue a small ribbon bow to the top.

To make these smart frames, cut two pieces of mounting board 25cm x 19cm (10in x 7½in). Cut a window 17cm x 11cm (7in x 4½in) in the centre of one piece. Cut two pieces of giftwrap to cover the frames. Lay the window mount on the wrong side of one piece and cut a window in the giftwrap, leaving a 2cm (¾in) margin. Snip to the corners and glue the margins down.

Cover the back of the frame with giftwrap, then cut two 1cm (⅜in) wide strips of mounting board 18cm (7¼in) long and one 22cm (8½in) long. Cover with paper and glue to the wrong side of the back just inside three of the edges. Spread glue on the strips and carefully place the front of the frame on top, checking that the outer edges are level.

Cut a rectangle of mounting board 18cm x 6cm (7¼in x 2¼in) for the stand. Score across the stand 5cm (2in) from one end. Cover the stand with giftwrap and glue the scored end to the back with the other end level with either a long or short side depending on whether your photo is in landscape or portrait form. Bend the stand outwards.

Drop two or three colours onto the water and swirl together with the end of a paint brush. Cut plain paper to fit the tray. Wearing rubber gloves, start at one end of the tray and lower the paper onto the surface of the water so it can pick up the pattern. Carefully lift up the paper.

Leave the paper to dry overnight on newspaper. You can remove the paint from the tray by drawing strips of newspaper across the surface of the water.

Now you are ready to cover your gift. Cut a rectangle of marbled paper large enough to wrap around the book with a 2.5cm (1in) margin on all sides. Wrap the paper around the book, open the cover and glue the paper inside the opening edges.

Prop up the book so the cover is open at a right angle. Snip the paper each side of the spine and stick the top and bottom margin inside the covers, folding under the corners.

For that extra special gift, cover a plain diary or note book in hand-marbled paper. Fill a shallow tray with water. Put spots of enamel paint on the water with a paint brush. If they sink the paint is too thick and needs thinning with a little white spirit. If they disperse into a faint film it is too thin and should be mixed with more paint.

Push the paper at the ends of the spine between the spine and the pages with the points of a pair of scissors. Arrange jewellery stones on the cover and use a strong glue to stick them in place. Cut two pieces of paper to fit inside the covers and glue inside.

Use the traditional art of quilling to make this attractive gift box a gift in itself. Cut coloured paper strips 4mm ($^3/_{16}$in) wide and about 20cm (8in) long. Scratch the end of a strip to soften the paper. Now coil the strip tightly between your thumb and finger. Release the coil so it springs open and glue the end against one side.

The coils can be gently squeezed into various shapes to fit your chosen design. Experiment with forming different shapes such as triangles and teardrops. To make smaller coils, cut shorter paper strips.

Draw a design on the lid of a wooden box and spread paper glue on a section of the lid. Arrange the coils on the glue and then move onto the next section. Fill in the whole design – any gaps around the motif can be filled with coils that match the colour of the box.

Transform ordinary pencils into these smart covered ones with scraps of wrapping paper. Choose round rather than hexagonal-shaped pencils. Cut a strip of wrapping paper wide enough to wrap around the pencil and as long as the pencil. Spray the back heavily with spray glue and wrap around the pencil.

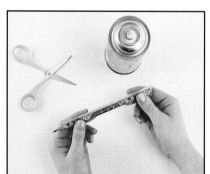

To finish, simply trim away the excess at the end of the pencil with a pair of small scissors.

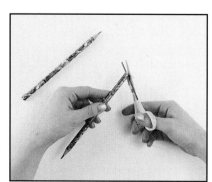

There is no excuse for mislaying letters with this smart letter rack. From thick mounting board cut a rectangle 24cm x 8cm (9¹/₂in x 3¹/₄in) for the front and 24cm x 10cm (9¹/₂in x 4in) for the back. Diagonally trim away the top corners and cover one side of each piece with giftwrap.

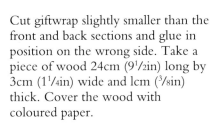

Cut giftwrap slightly smaller than the front and back sections and glue in position on the wrong side. Take a piece of wood 24cm (9¹/₂in) long by 3cm (1¹/₄in) wide and 1cm (³/₈in) thick. Cover the wood with coloured paper.

Cut a rectangle of mounting board 27cm x 7cm (10¹/₂in x 2³/₄in) for the base and cover with coloured paper. Use a strong glue to stick the front to one narrow edge of the wood keeping the lower edges level. Glue the back to the other side in the same way. Finish the letter rack by gluing this upper section centrally to the base.

Make this carrier bag and you have a gift bag for your presents or go a step further and make the bag itself the present. Cut a piece of thick yellow cardboard 57.5cm x 29cm (22⁵/₈in x 11¹/₂in). Refer to the diagram on page 96 and score along the solid and broken lines. Cut away the lower right-hand corner and cut into the base along the solid lines.

Fold the bag forwards along the solid lines and backwards along the broken lines. Turn the bag over and, with a pencil, lightly divide the front into quarters. Cut out a small hole at the centre for the clockwork. Cut out four pieces of red paper 1.5cm x 1cm (⁵/₈in x ³/₈in) and glue on the divisions 7cm (2³/₄in) from the hole.

Rub out the pencil lines. Join the side seam by gluing the narrow tab under the opposite end. Fold under the small base sections then glue the long sections underneath. Cut two strips of green cardboard for handles 30cm x 1cm (12in x ³/₈in). Glue the ends inside the top of the bag. Insert the clockwork rod through the hole and attach the hands.

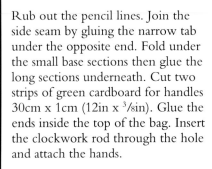

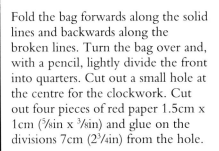

Paint a plain ceramic honey pot and transform it it into something striking for a unique gift. Using a fine paint brush and black ceramic paint, paint some bees on to the lid of the pot. If you are worried about painting free-hand, first draw the bees on with a chinagraph pencil. And if you are not even sure how to draw a bee, get a picture of one to copy.

Now paint the stripes with black ceramic paint. If, like this one, your pot is ridged, use the raised surface as a guide for your lines of paint. Otherwise you can use strips of masking tape to mask off those areas which are to be yellow. In order not to smudge the work, you may find it easier to paint the lower half first and then leave it to dry before painting the top half.

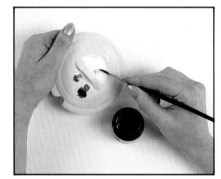

When all the black has dried, apply the yellow ceramic paint, carefully filling in the bee's striped body with a fine brush. Fill the pot with honey and have a nice breakfast!

Clowns are a very bright and jolly popular image and, painted on to wall plates like these, they make a colourful gift to decorate a child's room. Look at birthday cards, wrapping paper, toys and in children's books for inspiration.

Once you have drawn your design on paper, copy it on to a plate using a chinagraph pencil. When drawing your design, consider the shape of the plate; make the feet curl round the edge, as we have done here, and try to make the image fill as much of the plate as possible. Next, follow the chinagraph line with a line of black ceramic paint.

With a combination of ragging and flicking you can transform a plain china vase or jug into a work of art. You will need a piece of cloth for the ragging, a couple of fine artists' brushes and some ceramic paints. Dip the rag into one of the paints and then blot it onto some waste paper to remove any excess paint. Now begin to dab paint on to the vase.

Leave gaps between the dabs of paint to allow the background colour to show through. When you have evenly covered the surface, leave it to dry. Now spatter the vase with white ceramic paint, flicking the paint on with a fine brush. Once again, leave to dry.

Colour the main features such as clothes and hair using very bright ceramic paints: cherry red, lavender, blue, orange, yellow and green. Make the clothes colourful and busy, with plenty of spots, checks and patches.

Finally, fill in the background with circles, triangles or wavy lines, painted in brightly contrasting colours. When the paint has dried, finish off with a protective coat of ceramic varnish.

Finally, apply some gold ceramic paint with a fine paint brush, forming clusters of little gold dots across the surface of the vase. Be sure to clean your brush thoroughly in turpentine when you have finished.

# DECORATIVE DUCKS

M ade in the Phillipines from balsa wood, these lovely ornamental ducks are exported all over the world and are widely available in department stores. They are ideal for painting and make beautiful gifts. Draw your design on to the duck in pencil, either following one of the designs shown here or using a bird book as reference. Now start to paint.

Acrylic paints are ideal on this surface but you can also use glass or ceramic paints, or even a mixture of all three. Paint the main areas of colour first and then change to a finer brush and fill in details such as the eyes, the white ring round the neck and the markings on the wings and tail.

Finish off with a coat of polyurethane gloss varnish. If you have used a variety of paints remember that they will dry at different rates so make sure they are all dry before varnishing.

These jazzy potato printed cushions make inexpensive yet stylish gifts – you may even want to make some for your own home! Cut a potato in half and draw the design on to one half with a felt tip pen. Now cut around the motif so that the design stands proud of the background.

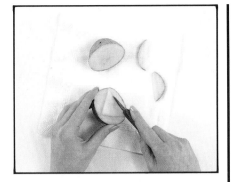

Paint some fabric paint on to the potato motif with a brush. Stamp off any excess paint on to some waste paper then print the motif on to your chosen fabric, leaving plenty of space for a second and even a third motif.

Cut another simple motif from the other half of the potato. Apply the colour as before and print on to the fabric. When the fabric has dried, iron on the back to fix the paints. Your fabric is now ready to be made up into cushions, curtains, blinds and so forth.

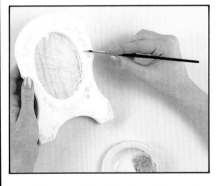

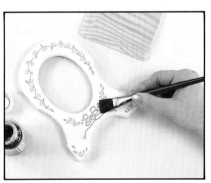

This pretty hand-painted frame is an ideal gift. Firstly, sand the frame until it is smooth and then give it a coat of white acrylic paint. Apply a second coat of paint if necessary and, when dry, draw the design with a soft pencil. Paint the design using acrylic paint in soft blues and greys with the flower centres in bright yellow.

Remove the backing and the glass and give the frame a protective coat of polyurethane varnish.

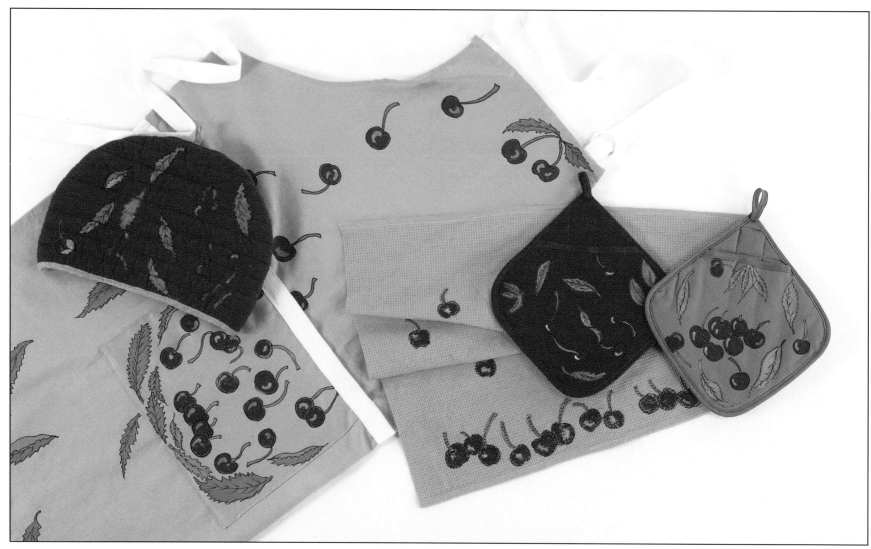

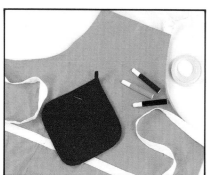

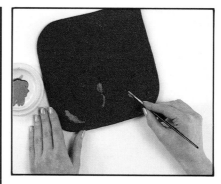

Decorate kitchen ware with a simple but effective design of cherries for a unique gift. You will need some fabric felt tip pens and/or some opaque fabric paint plus an apron, tea cosy, pot holder and tea towel to decorate.

Practise the design on some paper first, then, when you are confident, use a fine fabric felt tip pen to draw the outline of your design on to the fabric. Here, the leaves and cherries have been spaced out so that they appear to be tumbling down from the tree. On the apron pocket the leaves are grouped to act as a nest for the falling cherries.

Now fill in the outlines with red and green paint. On dark backgrounds you will need to use opaque paints; these are harder to apply than the felt tip pens, so be patient and keep going over the design to achieve the intensity of colour desired.

When the paint is dry, use the black felt tip pen to add veins to the leaves and shading to the cherries. To complete the design, add white highlights to the cherries. this can be done either with a pin or with the opaque fabric paint. Finally, iron the back of the fabric to fix the paints.

Open out the leg seams and sew the boot to the leg along E-D-E. Then fold the boot with right sides facing and sew the front to the side body along seam G-E on both sides, ensuring that point A matches. Sew seam E-F in black thread.

Close the back seam from G to C, leaving a gap for turning. Sew the boot soles into place. Turn the body the right way out and stuff firmly. Ladder stitch the back opening closed and place the body to one side.

For the jacket, join the two halves together by sewing seam L-M-L. Sew the sleeves to the jacket along J-K-J, easing to fit. Sew a strip of white fur fabric 14cm x 4cm (5½in x 1½in) to the edge of the sleeves, keeping the right sides together. Fold the strip over the raw edge of the sleeve and sew down on the reverse side.

Fold the sleeves in half and sew up the side seam O-J-N on both sides. At the base of the jacket, sew a strip of white fur fabric 42cm x 4cm (16½in x 1½in). Fold the strip back over the raw edge of the jacket and sew into place on the reverse side.

## MATERIALS

*Red velvet or felt*
*Black felt*
*Pink or flesh coloured felt*
*Very long white fur fabric*
*Short white fur fabric, for pom pom*
*Ribbon*
*Filling*

Delight the kids with this charming Santa doll. Size up the pattern overleaf and cut out all the pieces in the appropriate fabrics. For the body, sew the inside legs to the front body from A to B on either side. With right sides together, join the front body with attached legs to the side body from point D to C, matching point B. Repeat for the other side.

For the hood, turn up a narrow double hem on each short side. Sew a strip of white fur fabric 23cm x 4cm (9¼in x 1½in) to the front edge in the same way as for the jacket. Fold the hood in half and, with right sides together, sew seam P-Q.

Turn the hood the right way out and add a short piece of ribbon to each front corner of the hood. Fold down the point of the hood. Sew a running stitch around the edge of the pom pom and gather. Stuff gently, then pull the thread to gather tightly. Attach the pom pom to the side of the hood.

Place the pairs of arms right sides together and sew all around, leaving the top straight edges open. Turn and stuff the arms, then oversew arms to the body sides. Place the jacket on the body.

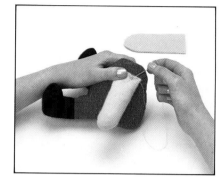

To make the head, sew up the darts on both head pieces. Place the two halves together with right sides facing and sew around the head, leaving the bottom straight edge open.

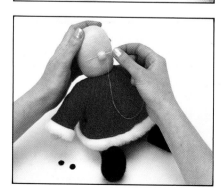

Turn the head the right way out. Place some filling into the head, stuffing it firmly. Gather the bottom edge of the head with a running stitch, then ladder stitch the head to the body.

Using a running stitch, gather the edge of the nose. Place a small amount of filling in the centre, then fasten off securely. Stitch the nose to the centre of the face. Cut two eye circles out of black felt and sew them into position above the nose.

Fold the side flaps of the long white hair piece down and sew seam R-S on either side. Sew the beard to the front of the hair piece from T to U on both sides. Turn the right way out and pull onto Santa's head so that the top of the beard just touches the nose. Stitch into place. Put the hood on Santa's head and tie into place under the beard.

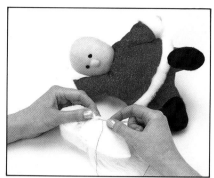

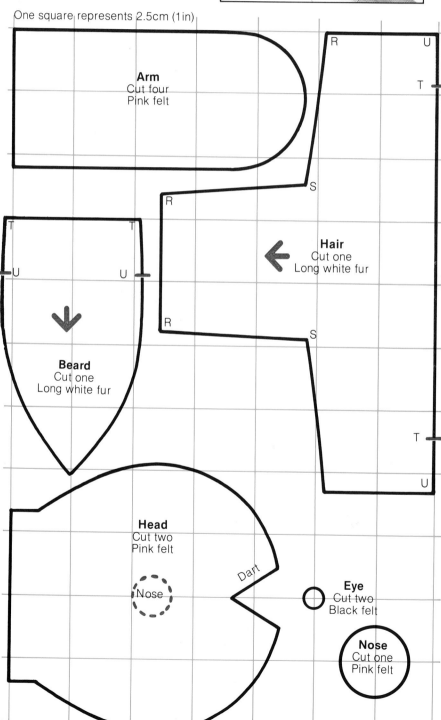

One square represents 2.5cm (1in)

**Arm**
Cut four
Pink felt

**Hair**
Cut one
Long white fur

**Beard**
Cut one
Long white fur

**Head**
Cut two
Pink felt

Nose

Dart

**Eye**
Cut two
Black felt

**Nose**
Cut one
Pink felt

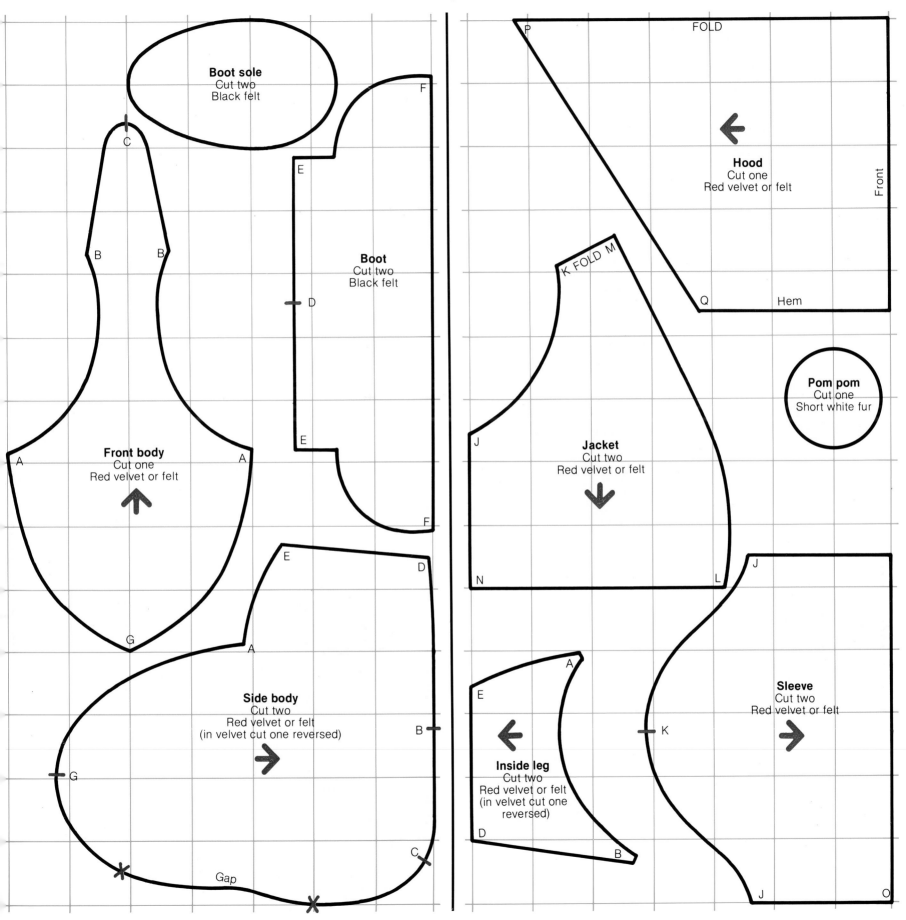

**Boot sole**
Cut two
Black felt

**Boot**
Cut two
Black felt

F

E

D

E

F

C

B    B

A                A

**Front body**
Cut one
Red velvet or felt

G

E                    D

A

**Side body**
Cut two
Red velvet or felt
(in velvet cut one reversed)

G

B

Gap

C

**Hood**
Cut one
Red velvet or felt

FOLD

Front

Hem

P

Q

**Pom pom**
Cut one
Short white fur

K FOLD M

J

**Jacket**
Cut two
Red velvet or felt

N                    L    J

**Sleeve**
Cut two
Red velvet or felt

K

J                O

A

E

**Inside leg**
Cut two
Red velvet or felt
(in velvet cut one
reversed)

D              B

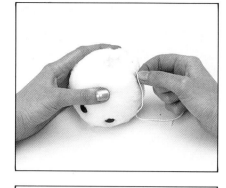

Pierce tiny holes in the eye positions and turn the head the right way out. Insert the safety eyes in the holes and secure on the reverse with metal washers. Stuff the head, shaping it into a round fat ball. Using a running stitch, gather the raw edge at the base and finish off securely.

Fold the nose piece in half and sew along the straight edge. Turn the right way out and stuff firmly. Gather the raw edge of the nose and finish off. Place this end on head at a central position between the eyes and ladder stitch firmly into place. Using black embroidery thread, stitch a 'V'-shaped mouth below the eyes. Then ladder stitch the head to the body.

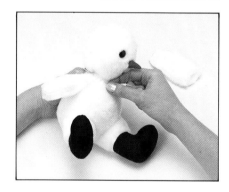

Place each pair of arms right sides together and sew all around, leaving the top straight edges open. Turn the arms the right way out and stuff them, adding far less filling to the top halves. Turn the raw edges in and oversew the arms into position on either side of the neck. Secure the hands to the body with a couple of stitches.

## MATERIALS

*Short pile white fur fabric*
*Black, red and green felt*
*Scrap of orange felt for nose*
*1 pair 13.5mm black safety eyes with metal washers*
*Black embroidery thread*
*Filling*

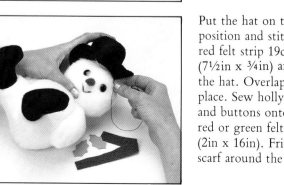

Sew the two hat brim pieces together around both the outer and inner edges. Fold the main body of the hat in half and sew around the short edge. Place the completed cylinder on top of the hat brim in a central position and oversew the two pieces together around the inner circle. Oversew the hat top into position and put some filling inside the hat.

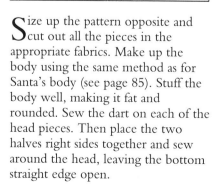

**S**ize up the pattern opposite and cut out all the pieces in the appropriate fabrics. Make up the body using the same method as for Santa's body (see page 85). Stuff the body well, making it fat and rounded. Sew the dart on each of the head pieces. Then place the two halves right sides together and sew around the head, leaving the bottom straight edge open.

Put the hat on the head in a lopsided position and stitch down. Wrap a red felt strip 19cm x 2cm (7½in x ¾in) around the base of the hat. Overlap ends and sew into place. Sew holly leaves onto the hat and buttons onto the body. Cut a red or green felt strip 5cm x 40cm (2in x 16in). Fringe the ends and tie scarf around the snowman's neck.

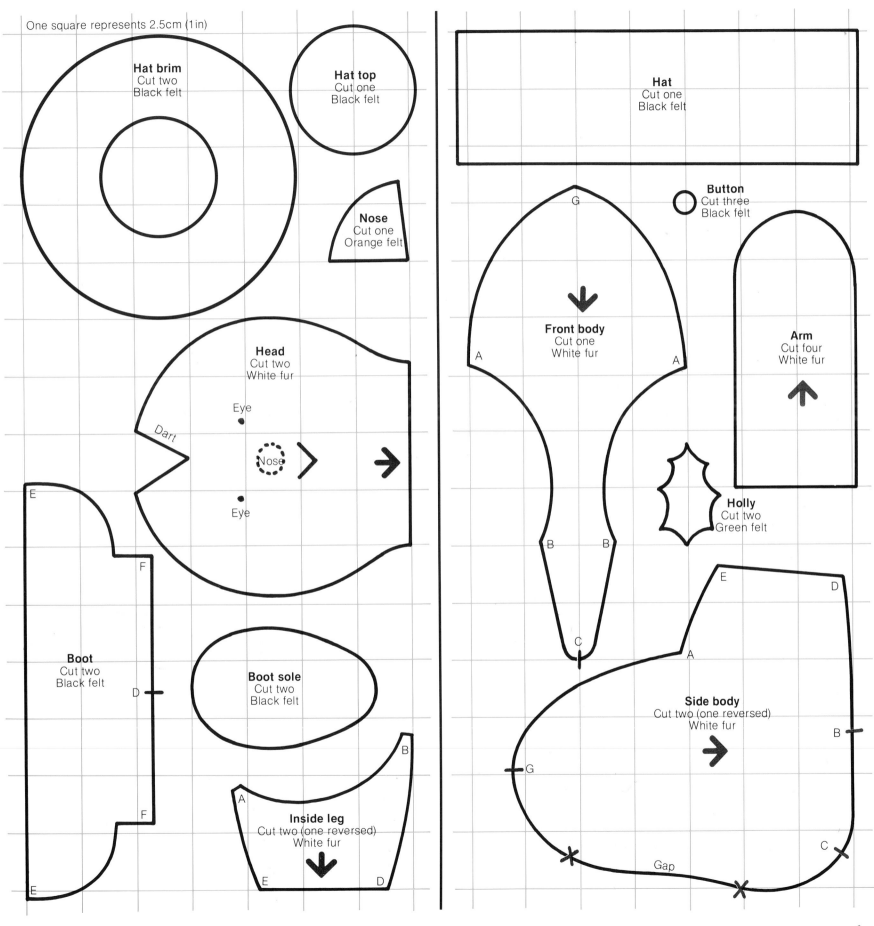

One square represents 2.5cm (1in)

**Hat brim**
Cut two
Black felt

**Hat top**
Cut one
Black felt

**Hat**
Cut one
Black felt

**Button**
Cut three
Black felt

**Nose**
Cut one
Orange felt

G

**Front body**
Cut one
White fur

A                    A

**Arm**
Cut four
White fur

**Head**
Cut two
White fur

Eye

Dart

Nose

Eye

B        B

**Holly**
Cut two
Green felt

E

F

**Boot**
Cut two
Black felt

D

F

C

E                    D

**Side body**
Cut two (one reversed)
White fur

B

**Boot sole**
Cut two
Black felt

A

**Inside leg**
Cut two (one reversed)
White fur

B

A

G

C

Gap

E                    D

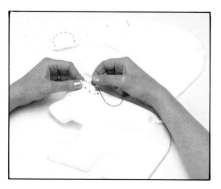

## MATERIALS

30cm (12in) white fur fabric
1 pair 13.5mm black safety
  eyes with metal washers
1 small plastic nose
Black embroidery thread
Filling

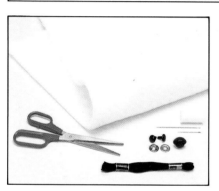

This charming toy will delight any child. Size up the pattern opposite and cut out all the pieces. Pierce a tiny hole at the eye position and cut a slit for the ears on each side body piece. Join both pieces of the inside body by sewing seam A-B, leaving a gap for turning and filling. Open out the inside body. Sew the under chin piece to the inside body along seam C-A-C.

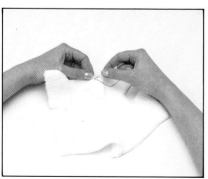

Sew up the darts at the rear of the side body pieces. Sew both halves of ears together, leaving the straight edge open. Turn the right way out and make a small tuck at the raw edge of the ear on both sides to curve the ear slightly inwards and oversew into place. Push the straight edge through the slit in the side body and sew the ears into position through all layers of fabric.

Join the head gusset piece to the side of the head on the side body piece by sewing seam J-K. Repeat on other side. Then sew up seam J-D at the front of the head.

Sew the inside body to the side body, starting at seam D-E. Then sew seam F-G and finally seam H-B. Repeat on other side.

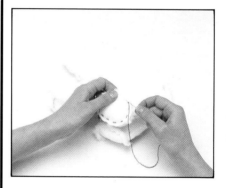

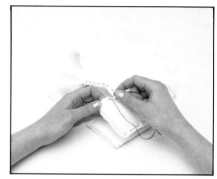

Fold the tail in half lengthwise. Sew along the curved edge, leaving the top open. Turn the tail, poking out the tip carefully. Sew seam K-B on the back of the bear, sewing in the tail at the same time where the two darts meet. Open out and stretch the bottoms of the feet and sew in the foot pads.

Turn the bear the right way out. Insert the safety eyes through the holes made earlier and secure on the reverse with metal washers. Poke a tiny hole at the very end of the snout and secure the plastic nose in the same way.

Fill the bear with stuffing, starting at the feet. Flatten the feet slightly as the filling is added. Mould the head shape by pushing more filling into the cheeks. When satisfied with the general shape of the bear, close the gap in the tummy using a ladder stitch.

With black embroidery thread, stitch through the feet four times on each paw to form claws. Using the same thread, embroider a smile on the bear's face. Finish off the mouth on either side with a small stitch at right angles to the main stitch.

Finally, taking a long needle and white thread, pull the eyes slightly together by passing the threaded needle from corner to corner of the opposite eyes, through the head. Fasten off securely.

**Side body**
Cut two (one reversed)
White fur

Dart

Tail

B

G

F

Ear

K

Eye

D

A

C  C

**Under chin**
Cut one
White fur

D

J

E

One square represents 2.5cm (1in)

B

**Inside body**
Cut two (one reversed)
White fur

H

Gap

G

F

**Foot pad**
Cut four
White fur

A
C

E

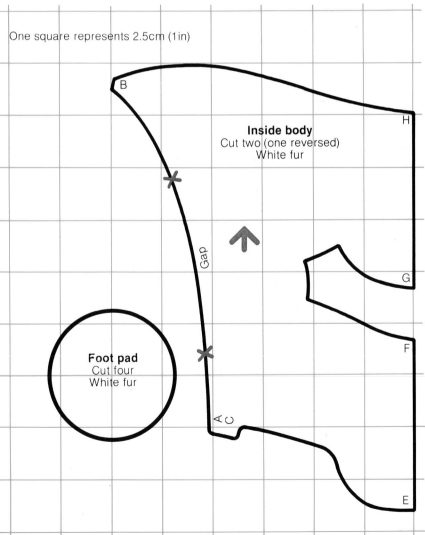

K

**Head gusset**
Cut one
White fur

J

**Tail**
Cut one
White fur

**Ear**
Cut four
White fur

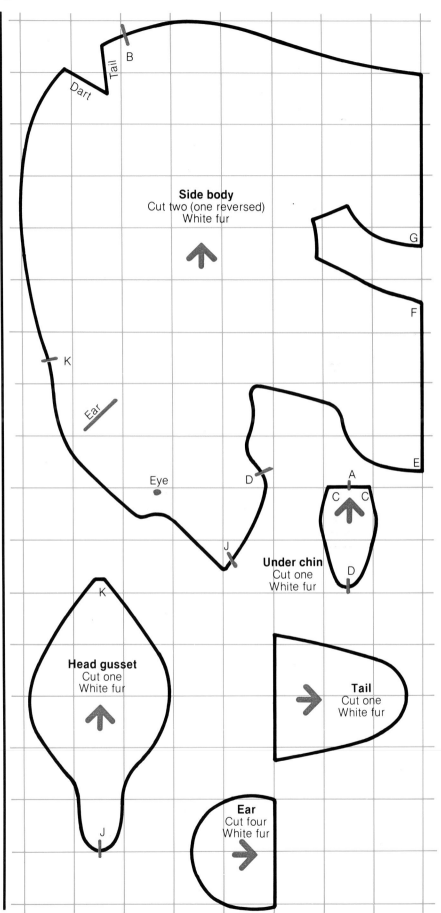

# TEMPLATES

Size up the templates on the following pages as follows: draw up a grid of 2.5cm (1in) squares, then copy the design onto your grid, square by square, using the grid lines as a guide.

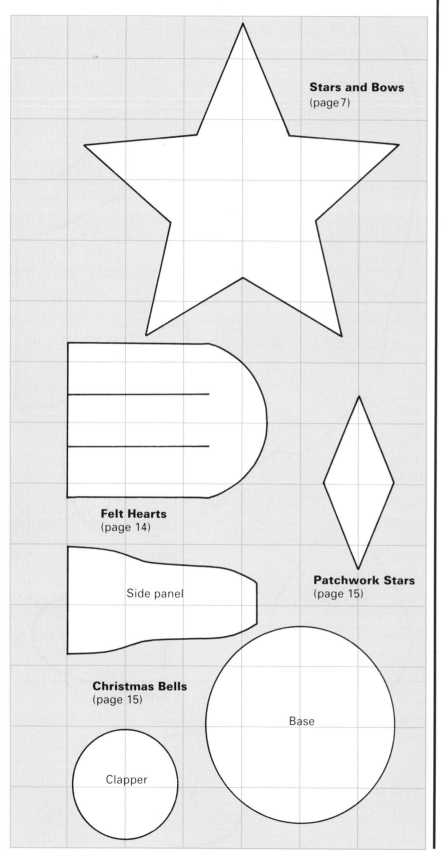

**Stars and Bows**
(page 7)

**Felt Hearts**
(page 14)

**Patchwork Stars**
(page 15)

Side panel

**Christmas Bells**
(page 15)

Base

Clapper

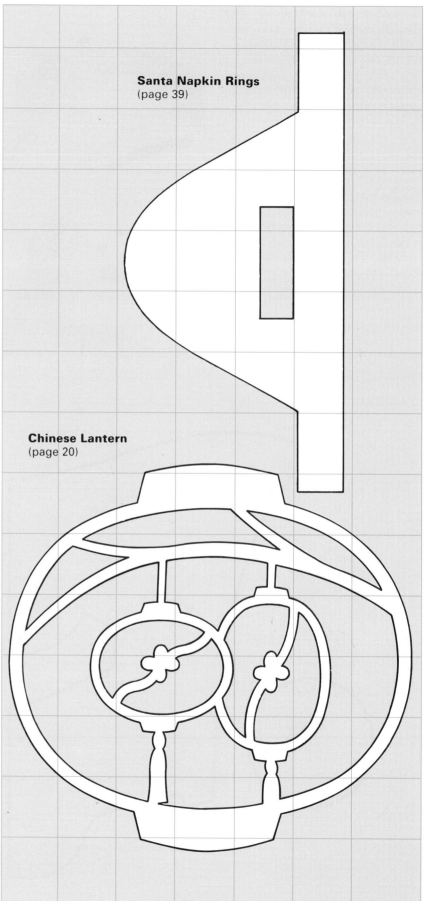

**Santa Napkin Rings**
(page 39)

**Chinese Lantern**
(page 20)

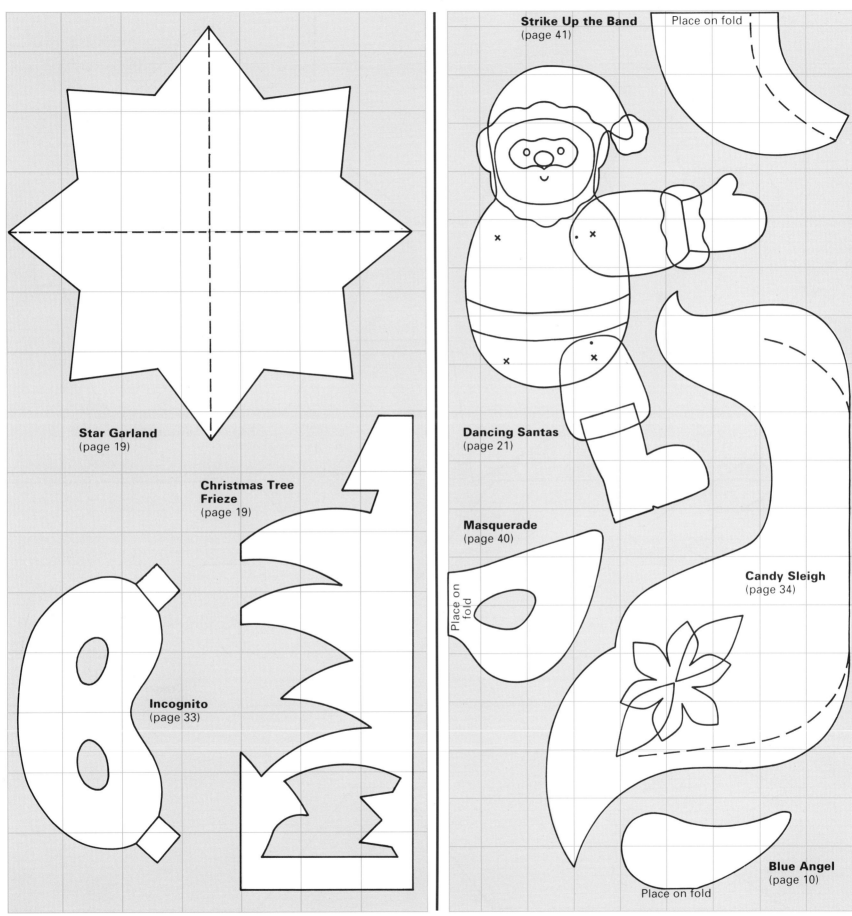

**Star Garland**
(page 19)

**Christmas Tree Frieze**
(page 19)

**Incognito**
(page 33)

**Strike Up the Band**
(page 41)

Place on fold

**Dancing Santas**
(page 21)

**Masquerade**
(page 40)

Place on fold

**Candy Sleigh**
(page 34)

**Blue Angel**
(page 10)

Place on fold

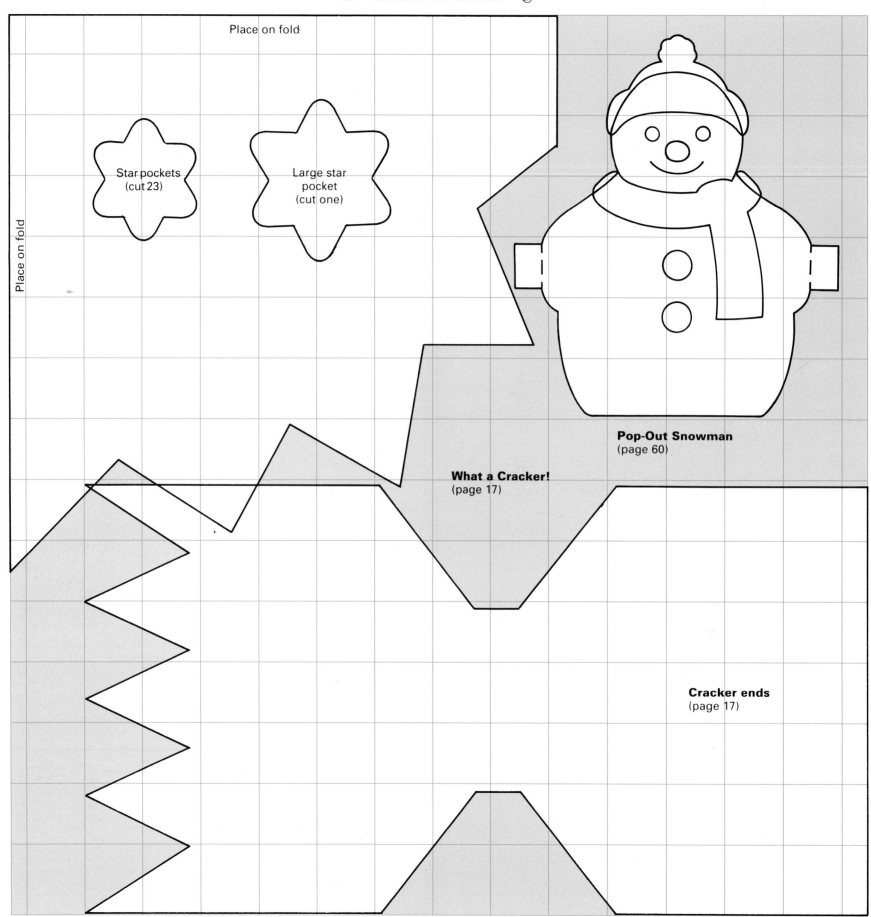

Place on fold

Place on fold

Star pockets
(cut 23)

Large star
pocket
(cut one)

**Pop-Out Snowman**
(page 60)

**What a Cracker!**
(page 17)

**Cracker ends**
(page 17)

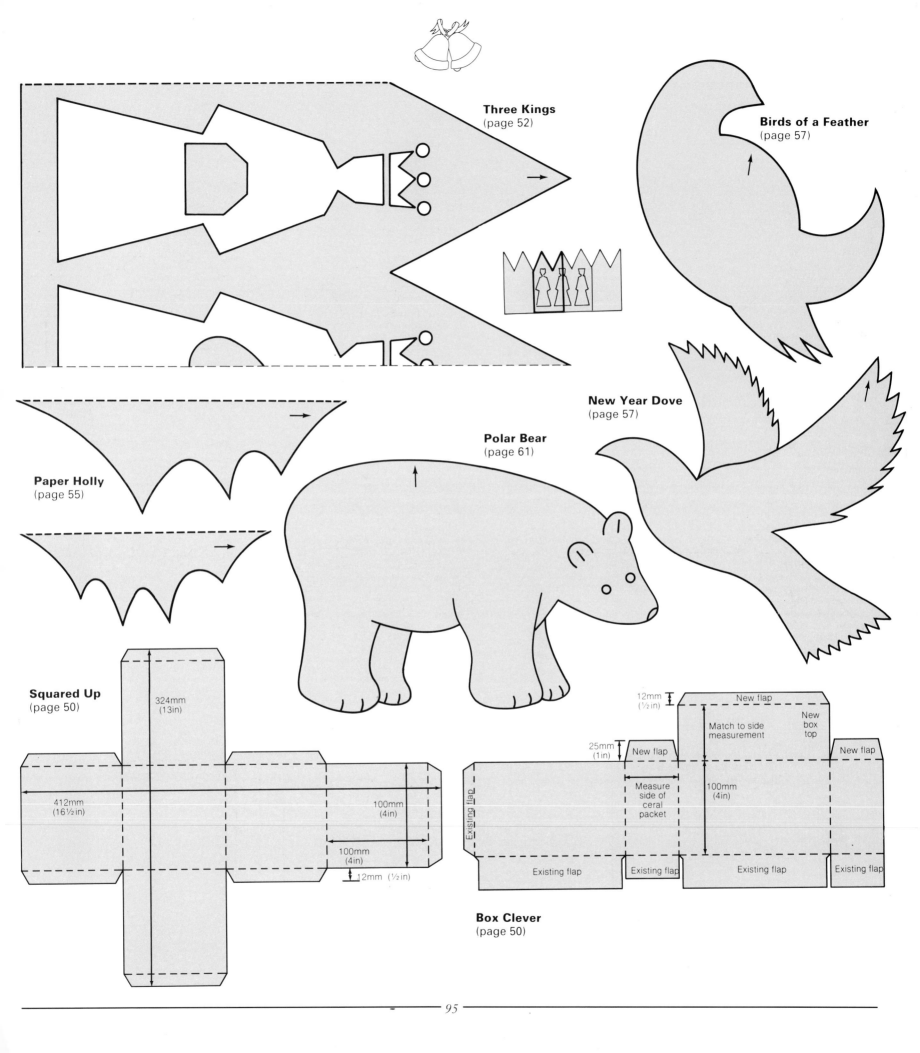

**Three Kings**
(page 52)

**Birds of a Feather**
(page 57)

**New Year Dove**
(page 57)

**Polar Bear**
(page 61)

**Paper Holly**
(page 55)

**Squared Up**
(page 50)

324mm
(13in)

412mm
(16½in)

100mm
(4in)

100mm
(4in)

12mm (½in)

**Box Clever**
(page 50)

12mm
(½in)

New flap

New box top

25mm
(1in)

New flap

Match to side measurement

New flap

Existing flap

Measure side of ceral packet

100mm
(4in)

Existing flap

Existing flap

Existing flap

Existing flap

# INDEX

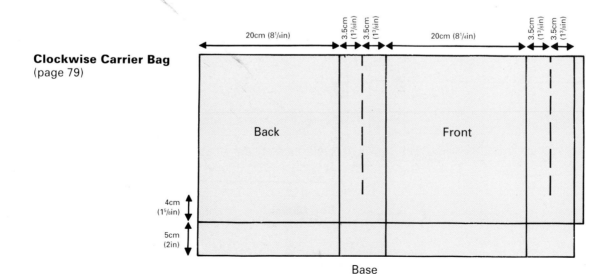

**Clockwise Carrier Bag**
(page 79)

20cm (8¼in)   3.5cm (1⅜in)   3.5cm (1⅜in)   20cm (8¼in)   3.5cm (1⅜in)   3.5cm (1⅜in)

Back          Front

4cm (1⅝in)

5cm (2in)

Base